# Praise for *Don't Look Down!*

"This isn't your typical business book—it's a rollicking, funny, and deeply human story of a man who built his life the hard way, and loved every minute of it."

—**SUSAN DELL'OSSO**, president, River Islands Development, LLC, Lathrop, California

"Campana shows that entrepreneurship isn't about having a master plan—it's about figuring it out as you go. A must-read for anyone on that path."

—**JOHN DUARTE**, president, Duarte Nursery, Modesto, California, and former US representative from California

"Campana's storytelling crackles with energy, insight, and wit. A compulsively readable journey through one entrepreneur's very human path to success."

—**GIUSEPPE GIORGIANNI**, founder and CEO, iNNOVA, Messina, Sicily

"If you've ever tried to build something from scratch—or thought about trying—this book is for you. Practical, honest, and refreshingly no-BS."

—**TERRANCE P. WITHROW**, CPA and Stanislaus County (California) Supervisor

"Bob Campana doesn't preach—he shares. His lessons come from decades of trial and error, making them all the more valuable."

—**JOE TRAINA**, founder and owner, The Fruit Yard, Modesto, California

"So many business books are theoretical. This one is lived. It's full of practical wisdom you can actually use."

—**JOSEPH SMITH**, president, Architecture
Plus, Inc., Modesto, California

"Whether it's a village in Thailand or a vineyard in France, Campana is always listening, learning, and connecting. That's the secret sauce."

—**FRANCESCO FRATANTONIO**, president, Principle
di Belmonte Hotel Group, Modica, Sicily

"Campana's life could have gone a dozen different ways. He chose the one with the steepest climb and the best view."

—**FRANK RATTO**, president, Ratto Bros., Inc., Modesto, California

"This book is the inspiration I need when the going gets hard. It delivers real-world business lessons with a storyteller's flair—like having a smart, funny mentor in my corner."

—**JOAQUIN RODRIGUEZ**, president, 3King Productions,
Manteca, California

"I thought I knew all the stories. Turns out, he saved a few for the book. I'm not sure whether to laugh, cry, or ground him."

—**DIANE CAMPANA**, author's mother

# DON'T LOOK DOWN!

*The* Improbable Adventures *and*
Battle-Tested Lessons *of a* Serial Entrepreneur

# DON'T LOOK DOWN!

## BOB CAMPANA

*with* NILES HOWARD

GREENLEAF
BOOK GROUP PRESS

Published by Greenleaf Book Group Press
Austin, Texas
www.gbgpress.com

Distributed by Greenleaf Book Group

For ordering information or special discounts for bulk purchases, please contact Greenleaf Book Group at PO Box 91869, Austin, TX 78709, 512.891.6100.

Design and composition by Greenleaf Book Group
Cover design by Greenleaf Book Group

Publisher's Cataloging-in-Publication data is available.

Print ISBN: 979-8-88645-398-0

eBook ISBN: 979-8-88645-399-7

To offset the number of trees consumed in the printing of our books, Greenleaf donates a portion of the proceeds from each printing to the Arbor Day Foundation. Greenleaf Book Group has replaced over 50,000 trees since 2007.

Printed in the United States of America on acid-free paper

25 26 27 28 29 30 31 32    10 9 8 7 6 5 4 3 2 1

First Edition

# CONTENTS

# Preface

The fluorescent lights at San Francisco International assaulted my jet-lagged senses as I staggered off the Pan Am 747 that late April afternoon in 1975. The six-hour flight from JFK had been quiet, the cabin dim, but I hadn't slept a wink. After five months lugging a thirty-pound backpack through Asia and two months of relentless bacillary dysentery, I was worn to the bone. Thirty pounds lighter than when I'd started, I was a ghost of myself, muscles gone, clothes hanging from my shoulders, mind fogged by exhaustion—and, frankly, by wonder. All I could think about was finding a soft bed.

Knowing that the airport's terminal would be a crush of traffic, I'd phoned ahead to Aunt Hazel, asking her to meet me a mile away in the Millbrae Square Shopping Center parking lot. Crossing the pedestrian walkway over the Bayshore Freeway, I glanced down at the cars stacked bumper to bumper, inching out of the city in evening traffic. It was an everyday scene, but that day, the sight was surreal, almost alien. In recent months, I'd been in places where people were grateful to travel by any means available—crowded buses, hand-me-down bicycles, even on foot. And here I was, back in a land of freeways, filled with drivers in private cars, moving slowly but moving all the same. I felt a surge of gratitude to be born in a place where opportunity felt almost woven into the air. My pulse quickened as I made a quiet vow to make use of the doors this country held open.

The vibrant streets of Jakarta and New Delhi, the smiles of rice farmers, and the tranquil waters of Kathmandu had opened my eyes to the vastness of humanity—and nudged me to understand my place in it. For some, the sheer scale of it all might have felt overwhelming, even disheartening. For me, it was a shot of adrenaline. Actually, it was more like an IV drip. I was that kid in the proverbial candy store, bursting with energy but uncertain where to channel it.

In the beginning, my path was anything but straight. I stumbled forward, nudged by family encouragement, a few foolish decisions, and a handful of mentors who pointed out which cliffs not to jump off. There was no grand plan, no master design; it was less like joining a high-speed freeway and more like bouncing along unfamiliar blue highways, making wrong turns, nervously checking the gas gauge, wondering where the next pit stop might be. I picked up sales, finance, and management skills as I went, through reading and plenty of trial and error—emphasis on the error. Some days were a grind; others were hair-raising and exhilarating.

My entrepreneurial journey was nothing if not winding. Each day brought its own mix of happenstance, risk-taking, "aha" moments, despair, and excitement. My right brain and left brain seemed locked in a constant, sometimes combative dialogue. Building hot tubs and swimming pools revealed a knack for salesmanship I hadn't realized I had, and this eventually opened the door to an artistic side I didn't even know existed. In my forties, I took on helicopter piloting—a skill that balanced total freedom with something closer to military discipline. A disastrous first attempt at the restaurant business didn't stop me from trying again, and the second try led to one of the most popular dining spots in Central California. Nothing about my path was linear; each venture bled into the next, blending together in ways I could never have anticipated. Even now, at seventy, new opportunities appear, revealing more layers of this ever-evolving mix that makes up my life.

As part of this incredible journey, I married the woman of my dreams and raised four happy, smart, and generous daughters. I soared over mountains and plains, stared down crocodiles in the outback, dined in five-star Italian restaurants, and was inducted into the ancient Order of the Dragon by a blood descendant of Count Dracula himself. I developed close relationships with people from all levels of society and corners of the world. These associations have enriched my life beyond measure. They have expanded my horizons, deepened my insight, and made me more empathetic to the plights of others.

As I researched this book, I also learned more about my forebears, which helped me better understand the experiences that continue to shape my family. My ancestors' journeys from Italy to New York to San Francisco to the Sierra foothills required them to rebuild their lives from scratch. They realized and accepted that some things were within their control, while others were not, and learned to distinguish between the two. Seeing how they faced and overcame challenges has helped me better understand how change fosters resilience, empathy, and insight—the foundations of true wisdom.

My wife, Lynna, my anchor and wise critic, continually reminds me that age and experience don't automatically bring wisdom. But they do bring a greater appreciation for the journey, the people we meet, and the lessons along the way. These are gifts that shouldn't go to waste. That's why I'm here: to share with current and aspiring entrepreneurs what I've learned, help them find their own paths, and maybe even leave the world a little better than I found it.

Welcome to an incredible adventure.

# 1

# San Francisco

## The Entrepreneurial Mind

Entrepreneurs are like immigrants: They hunger for independence and the opportunity to own their destiny. They seek to live on their own terms, unencumbered by conventional expectations. They shake off the constraints of tradition and bureaucracy. They eagerly take risks, face challenges, and bounce back from soul-crushing setbacks. That spirit runs deep in my family history. It is my lucky inheritance.

My paternal great-grandparents came to America from Italy with little more than a dream and the guts to chase it. Their son, my grandfather, ditched a steady job during the Great Depression to start his own business. My father made a gutsy decision to shutter the family business, pull up stakes, and start a better life in the Sierra foothills. Their stories fill me with admiration and gratitude. They remind me daily that anything is possible if you put your heart, mind, and soul into it. They push me onward.

John Campana, his wife, Mary Victoria Iona, and their infant son, Dominik, left Catanzaro, Italy, a small city in the southern region of Calabria, by steamship in 1902. They fled poverty and political unrest. It was a four-thousand-mile odyssey to a strange land populated by people speaking an unfamiliar tongue. They endured cramped and unsanitary steerage conditions and faced impertinent questions and potential rejection by uniformed officers at Ellis Island. But they trusted that luck, perseverance, and hard work would help them survive and prosper.

Instead of settling among the tenements of Little Italy or the crowded streets of East Harlem, they took a northbound train into the heart of upstate New York, where the landscape opened to wide rivers and factory towns tucked between hills. They settled in Rome, a modest, industrious city in Oneida County, where opportunity, though elusive, was at least on offer. John found work in a brass mill, shoveling coal into the roaring furnaces—a task no doubt as exhausting as it was dangerous. It was nothing to brag about but paid enough to secure a mortgage on a small house in the Italian quarter.

The Campanas lived at the intersection of two worlds, balancing the pull of their heritage and the push of their new homeland. In school, the children stumbled over English idioms and playground slang, their accents marking them as different. Little by little, they adjusted—learning not only how to speak the language but also how to wear it like a second skin.

In 1922, John and Mary packed their belongings, gathered their children, and boarded a train west. Booming postwar San Francisco promised not only better weather but also fresh opportunities for Italian Americans. It was another daunting move—twenty-five hundred miles across the country to a city they knew only by reputation—but after years of scraping by on the East Coast, a chance worth taking.

Train tickets were expensive—$50 a person, a small fortune for a family of eleven—but they managed it by selling what they could and leaving the rest behind. The five-day journey was no small feat with nine children in tow. There was little rest in the stiff coach seats, and keeping the younger ones entertained for days on end felt like an endurance test.

They jammed into a small apartment at 1845 Mason Street, between Russian Hill and the Italian mecca of North Beach, and settled in as best they could. John took a job as a janitor at the Federal Reserve Bank, cleaning marble floors and brass railings. The oldest child, Dominik, called Don, sold meat for Armour & Company, the giant meatpacking company out of Chicago, making his rounds to the small grocers and delis that lined the Italian markets of North Beach.

In 1928, Don married Helen Rosalie Mendler, the spunky twenty-three-year-old daughter of a German-born brewery worker. They rented a bungalow at 939 Plymouth Avenue, on the southwest edge of the city in Oceanview, a working-class neighborhood where gardens and chicken coops were as common as front porches. The house was small but had enough space for the life they wanted to build.

On October 29, 1929, known as Black Tuesday, the US stock market experienced a catastrophic crash, marking the beginning of the Great Depression. My father, Robert, was three months old. Somehow my grandfather's energy, wit, and resourcefulness kept him employed as a salesman for Armour & Co. His job involved delivering sausages, ham, and smoked delicacies from the company's plant on Battery Street. More importantly, it required building trust with owners of delicatessens and small grocery stores, many of whom were also first- or second-generation Italian immigrants. He was well suited to the task. His outgoing, charismatic personality won him many friends. He had more than a knack for sales—he had an instinct for seeing the bigger picture.

My grandfather was compact and rotund, with a ruddy complexion and an animated manner—people likened him to New York City's mayor Fiorello La Guardia, the energetic "Little Flower" who charmed and invigorated the Big Apple during the Depression. Don approached business like an entrepreneur, taking risks, building connections, and turning small wins into bigger opportunities. He treated his route like a business, thought strategically about expanding his territory, and spotted opportunities others overlooked. Not surprisingly, Armour's archrival Hormel hired him in 1937 to help introduce a new canned pork product called Spam, a cheap, convenient protein that needed no refrigeration; it was perfect for financially stressed households, and sales soared. The experience gave him the financial resources and confidence for what would come next. My grandmother Helen once told me, "We needed plenty of both."

In 1940, the Don J. Campana Co. opened in a small, rented cold-storage warehouse in an alley off Minna Street between Third and Fourth in the South of Market district. It was a neighborhood of printing companies, machine shops, and single-room hotels. It was farther away from the North Beach Italian community, but the rent was lower.

In retrospect, it was an ambitious, if not foolhardy, undertaking. Don not only competed with other mom-and-pop distributors but also with the much bigger and well-established purveyor Molinari & Sons. Why did he think he could survive in that cutthroat arena?

It's hard to know. But San Francisco was growing fast, and I can only surmise that he figured his deep relationships with deli owners gave him an edge.

It was tough going. Every weekday before sunrise, Don loaded his GMC panel truck with the day's orders and blocks of ice to keep them fresh. Sometimes, his younger brothers Frank, Sam, Ned, or Angelo pitched in, but they had other jobs, and he often had no other company than the occasional stray cat.

Looking back eighty years later, I marvel at the guts it took to start that business. As someone who has built my own companies, I know how it feels to build something from nothing and how isolating it can be. Entrepreneurship may be freeing, but it's a heavy freedom. The weight of every decision falls on your shoulders.

Don wore many hats—buyer, logistics guy, salesman, and problem-solver, with no real divide between business and family life. Helen kept the books, sent out invoices to customers they trusted with credit, and made sure the bills got paid.

Bringing in prosciutto, Parmigiano-Reggiano, and salami by ship from Italy wasn't easy or cheap. Dealing with overseas suppliers involved correspondence via letter or telegram. Don and Helen had to coordinate every purchase, shipment, and customs form to ensure everything arrived on time and met US laws. Shipping was so slow and unpredictable that they constantly ran out of one thing or another.

After Pearl Harbor, further chaos ensued. Products from Italy became hard to get, forcing Don to find local producers able to mimic traditional Italian methods. Rationing added another complication. But war also created opportunity. With men deployed, working women sought the kind of convenient, shelf-stable, and prepared products that Italian markets offered.

After World War II, the Don J. Campana Co. grew rapidly.

With soldiers home and consumer spending on the rise, Americans developed a taste for international foods like salami, sausages, and cheeses. San Francisco's Italian American community had more disposable income, eating out more often and buying specialty products. Granddad seized the opportunity. He expanded his product line; established supplier relationships with upscale restaurants, hotels, and supermarkets; and scaled his operations to meet growing demand.

He invested in new trucks, hired employees, and increased his visibility in San Francisco's business community. Stability also allowed him to deepen his involvement in civic and social organizations. He became active in the Calamari Club, a business group focused on Italian American connections. He became a life member of the Freemasons, an organization committed to personal growth and community service. He took a leadership role in the Shriners, focusing on children's healthcare. He actively participated in the Elks Lodge, supporting veterans and local charity efforts.

All this networking was undoubtedly good for business, but I like to think it was more than that. It was about strengthening human relationships, earning trust, and giving back—core principles that matter as much in business as in life. These values shaped how he interacted with employees, partners, and customers, underscoring a belief that business success was about more than profits.

My father absorbed these lessons, though he approached life differently. He shared the understanding that business is about making a meaningful impact on the community and the world. That belief filtered down to me as well. Throughout my career, relationships, trust, and giving back have been guiding principles. Supporting causes, engaging with the community, and building strong connections haven't just enriched my life—they've also been key to my success.

Every generation is shaped by its times. My grandfather, who grew up in a rough-and-tumble world and started his career in the go-go 1920s, saw life as an arena for bold moves—where fortune favored those willing to dive in, take chances, and weather setbacks without hesitation. To him, risk was just part of the game, a necessary ingredient for success, and he embraced it with grit, knowing there were always opportunities around the corner if you hustled hard enough.

My father, molded by the memory of the Depression, was keenly aware that things could spin out of control without warning. Daily life was strongly affected by faraway events and random tides. He preferred known ground to uncertain heights. Where my grandfather moved boldly, my father measured his steps. Easygoing and good-humored, he sought to minimize conflict and avoid unnecessary risks.

After graduating from Abraham Lincoln High School, located on the west side of the city, Dad enlisted in the Navy, just as the war was ending. The military, scaling back, offered not the thrill of distant battles but the promise of structure. He imagined orders to the sunny South Pacific—palm trees, open skies, and a taste of adventure. Instead, he shuffled papers on Treasure Island, a man-made speck in San Francisco Bay. Though it suited his demeanor, he once confided to me that the assignment left him with a nagging sense of missing out on something bigger. "I told people I served on an island in the Pacific," he once said. "It was technically true, or close enough." Was that an admission or a joke? I wasn't sure, and I'm not sure he was either.

After leaving the Navy in 1950, Dad settled into a job at his father's company, which had grown to 150 commercial accounts around the Bay Area. It had a half dozen trucks on the move daily: Dad drove one, his younger brother Richard another, and a distant relative I called Uncle Nick a third. There was also a rowdy bunch of hired hands.

At age twenty-one, Dad courted a teenage Treasure Island pool secretary. She came from money and looked it: fashionable clothes, a genteel manner, and an air of sophistication. Her parents, Ellsworth and Mildred Roberts, owned hundreds of acres of East Bay farmland developed into suburban neighborhoods and industrial zones after World War II. On Sunday, August 31, 1952, the society page of *The Oakland Tribune* contained the following item:

> The bride of Robert Don Campana of San Francisco since mid-August is the former Diane Clare Roberts of San Leandro, whose marriage took place at St. John's Church in San Leandro. Her father, Ellsworth G. Roberts, walked with her up the aisle, following her three attendants. Bridesmaids Mrs. Donald G. Boone and Barbara Ellison were in yellow and lavender ballerina-length dresses, each with the other's costume color repeated in her bouquet and headpiece of carnations.

The marriage was an unlikely union, a fusion of modest ambition and inherited wealth: he the twenty-three-year-old son of a second-generation Italian immigrant raised on hard work and pragmatism; she born into a world where money softened life's edges. There were whispers around the family about the Robertses selling off one big tract or another, and it didn't go unremarked that Diane's grandmother Minnie lived in a luxury high-rise overlooking Oakland's Lake Merritt. She also drove an expensive car. In any case, little wealth trickled down to our household.

Without going too deeply down a psychology rabbit hole, I've often wondered whether my parents' different life experiences had anything to do with my entrepreneurial passion. Did the interplay of those two worlds spark a competitive impulse? Did I want to prove I belonged in my mom's tony world? Or did I just want to drive a nice car like Minnie?

I came into this world on January 2, 1954. For the first five years of my life, we lived in a small apartment on a busy street in the suburb of Daly City, just south of the San Francisco line. It was a growing postwar suburb, with rows of modest, single-family homes built for returning veterans and young families seeking a fresh start.

With the impending arrival of their third child, my sister Laureen, my parents bought a three-bedroom concrete home in a new South San Francisco subdivision called Sunshine Gardens. South San Francisco was an industrial hub known for its factories, meatpacking plants, and an iconic hillside sign proclaiming it "The Industrial City." By the late 1950s, it was evolving into a residential suburb with new schools and parks. Sunshine Gardens was a peaceful enclave with modest ranch-style homes and small yards. It was a wholesome, working-class neighborhood in a *Leave It to Beaver* era. My small bedroom adjoined that of my parents. My sister Kathleen occupied the third bedroom, later sharing it when Laureen came along.

On Sundays, we'd often head back into the city and bond with assorted aunts, uncles, and cousins at the home of my dad's parents. Although the meat business was doing well, and they could afford something bigger, they lived on the first floor of a three-story building they owned, renting out two apartments above.

When the family assembled, food was plentiful. The aroma of fried garlic and smoky sausages floated through the Italian German household. Family gatherings were chaotic symphonies: kids whining and adults blustering about sports, business, and some relative's new baby. I couldn't wait to get back to Sunshine Gardens.

When I was seven years old, my grandfather died unexpectedly at age fifty-nine. My memory of the days surrounding his passing is blurry. I had no real conception of death and only a vague recollection of my grandfather as anything but a looming presence.

My grandfather's passing sent ripples through both the business and my family, affecting all in ways that I could not fully appreciate. For any founder-run company, suddenly losing its chief is a shock; a business built on relationships and personal trust relies heavily on its leader. There was no succession plan. My grandmother had no desire to step in full time, nor did she have the necessary contacts or credibility with Italian deli owners. The role fell to Dad. It was not a burden he wanted or was in any way prepared for.

Life in South San Francisco was secure and predictable. I played baseball with friends in the quiet streets and biked where I wanted. In grammar school, I was known as a happy-go-lucky prankster. One teacher, knowing Dad was in the meat business, asked me to get cow eyeballs for biology class. I brought them in a cardboard container, like a Kentucky Fried Chicken bucket. The orbs floated in blood. Not one to pass up an opportunity for mischief, I poured some down my arm, dropped to the floor, and screamed. A panicked teacher brought a cup of water from the bathroom and flooded my arm to find the source of the bleeding. She found . . . nothing. That little episode earned me a two-day suspension. It was not my first run-in with the education establishment, nor, unfortunately, the last.

My father, despite his reluctance to challenge authority, shared my iconoclasm about school. When I needed a parent's note to explain an absence, Dad wrote that I had contracted bubonic plague. "It was a frightening situation," he began, "but we luckily found a specialist from Tanzania who saved my son's life. We are so grateful for this miracle." The principal read it, peered unsmiling over her reading glasses, and silently gestured toward my classroom.

My fourth-grade teacher was a strict, squat woman who wore wool wraparound dresses, even on the warmest days. In my mind, she represented everything boring and stifling about the adult world. One day, she strode to the front of the room, her face gray, and grimly announced: "The president has been shot in Dallas." The air went heavy, the rowdy classroom silent. The outside world had forced its way into our safe suburban lives.

The next few days were a patchwork of somber images, with my parents glued to the black-and-white TV. Stone-faced newsmen droned in somber tones, a horse-drawn wagon carried a flag-draped coffin, the slain president's little boy stood next to his mom, saluting. I sensed that something fundamental had changed. The world wasn't as safe, orderly, or predictable as I had thought.

It would be a stretch to say that warm November week set the stage, planted the seed, or whatever analogy you want to use for everything that came after. I can't say it sparked in me a desire to grab control, to make sure my life was my own. I'll leave that kind of armchair psychology to others. But it undoubtedly influenced, in some small way, my perspective on life.

In junior high, I got into fights. A guy challenged me to meet him behind the parking lot after school. Classmates circled and cheered as we battled to a draw. This behavior did not go unnoticed by teachers or my parents. "I don't know what's gotten into you," my dad said one night. Was that a question? I didn't know. I just shrugged.

My grandmother, tired of keeping the books, began dating and married a rich widower from San Mateo named Kai Freitag. They moved to Woodside, California, an exclusive enclave south of San

Francisco, and seemed to play golf all the time. The woman at the center of our extended family suddenly belonged to a different world. It felt like she had moved on to something I wasn't fully part of.

Sometimes I drove with Dad to the firm's office. One of the Campana company's biggest clients was the Matson Steamship Company. Hazel, my grandmother Campana's sister, was the president's secretary. Matson's sleek, modern headquarters overlooked San Francisco Bay and the Embarcadero. From Aunt Hazel's window, I saw the SS *Lurline*, Matson's gleaming white passenger liner. The *Lurline* gained fame in the 1930s by ferrying celebrities and the well-to-do between San Francisco and Hawaii. By the early 1960s, it was nearing the end of that glamorous life due in part to Pan American World Airways' long-haul flights with Boeing's 707, but I didn't know that. Seeing the huge ship gave me a thrill.

I rode with my dad to the dock and watched longshoremen hoist our delicacies onto the ship as it prepared to head out under the Golden Gate Bridge and over the Pacific. I imagined the exotic adventures awaiting its passengers and wondered what it would be like.

On another day, Uncle Nick let me ride with him on deliveries. He had what my dad called the gift of gab. Having spent his childhood in Italy, he engaged old Italian deli owners in their native tongue using many hand gestures. I didn't understand what they said, but it was good-natured banter. The deli owners pointed to items in the display cases and handed Nick a list of items to bring on his next trip.

Hanging around the Campana warehouse and riding along on routes gave me an early glimpse of running a small business. The real action was not in fancy boardrooms, like in the movies, but on loading docks and storefronts surrounded by hanging salamis and cheese wheels. I soaked in the cadence of commerce, the nods of understanding between parties, the value of relationships.

But those experiences also revealed a side of life that my Sunshine Gardens friends never saw. Robbery was an ever-present threat. Uncle Nick kept a loaded revolver in his truck's glove compartment and tucked it into his jacket pocket when we stopped at delis in certain neighborhoods. A few shopkeepers paid cash, and the bad guys knew it. One day, a group of roughnecks crowded around us, demanding money. My uncle reached into his jacket pocket; the lurkers knew what was in there and backed off. "This is the real world," Uncle Nick said as we drove away. "You need to learn about it."

It was the hard underbelly of America. I gazed out the truck windows at men who failed in their lives and were trapped in a cycle of alcohol and drugs. I wondered how people in America could end up that way. It scared me.

San Francisco was changing. Hippies filled the streets around Haight-Ashbury. The so-called Summer of Love in 1967 also brought drugs, protests, and violence. The following year, someone shot and killed two high school students on a remote road north of the city. It was to be the first in a series of attacks by the Zodiac Killer.

I also sensed a mood change in our household. My parents became more subdued, my father's loud laugh less frequent, my mother's movements a little too quick. I felt a heaviness in the air. One night, half asleep, fretting no doubt about undone homework or fantasizing about a girl, I heard sharp voices through the thin drywall. The words were muffled, but the sentence fragments had a sharp edge:

" . . . we have to figure this out . . ."

" . . . there has to be a way . . ."

" . . . can't keep doing this . . ."

The meaning hovered just out of reach, but I knew it had something to do with money. My stomach churned. Psychologists say children sense when something disrupts the emotional balance of the household; it disturbs their sense of well-being. Lying in bed, I stared at the ceiling, feeling vulnerable and much older.

By 1968, the Don J. Campana Co. was a shell of the once-prosperous enterprise my grandfather had built. More people shopped at big supermarkets. Middle-class tastes continued shifting toward mass-market foods, and many young people rejected anything that sniffed of tradition. Traditional Italian meats and cheeses didn't fit the new gestalt. The small grocers and delis that supported the business were vanishing as owners died and leases expired.

The Campana building looked run down. Employees drifted away, laid off or lured by other opportunities. Uncle Richard, my dad's only sibling, moved to Santa Rosa to ride horses, or so the story went. (He later divorced his wife, married a woman in Indiana, managed a company that made industrial vent pipes, and died near South Bend in 2016 at the age of eighty-three.)

Industries, markets, and companies, like people, have a natural life cycle. There comes a time when business owners must make a tough decision: Ride it to the bottom or quit while there's still money in the bank. In the end, it wasn't a tough call for Dad. One evening, he came home from the city with some news. San Francisco was planning a big convention center in the South of Market neighborhood. The city was to condemn hundreds of homes and business buildings, including ours. "Maybe it isn't so bad," he said. "Things just aren't what they used to be. We're done."

Fortunately, at age forty, he had another option in his back pocket. He and I had been spending weekends building a log cabin on a little lot his mother bought in Murphys, a gold rush town in the scenic Sierra foothills. It was 150 miles by car but a thousand miles away from the pressures of city life. An appliance and furniture store there offered him a management job.

In January 1969, halfway through my freshman year at El Camino High School, the Don J. Campana Company closed for good. A "For Sale" sign appeared in the front yard of the little Sunshine Gardens house. A moving van pulled up out front, collected our stuff, and headed toward Murphys as we started a new life.

## Entrepreneurial Life Lessons

- Entrepreneurship may be freeing, but it's a heavy freedom. The weight of every decision falls on your shoulders.

- Networking is more than good business; it's about strengthening human relationships, earning trust, and giving back.

- Founder-run businesses need clear succession plans—it's an essential bridge to a lasting legacy.

- Industries, markets, and businesses have life cycles; knowing when to pivot or let go is a hallmark of wise leadership.

# 2

# Murphys

## Vision and Values

R unning a small business requires a basic grasp of finance, along with skills in operations, marketing, leadership, customer service, strategic planning, legal compliance, and time management. These skills are not innate; they are acquired through a combination of practical experience, mentorship, formal education, self-study, and learning from mistakes.

While essential, they aren't enough to build a successful enterprise—you need vision, resilience, adaptability, and the ability to inspire others through uncertainty and challenges. Those qualities arise from personality traits like curiosity, decisiveness, self-awareness, and empathy and core values such as gratitude, humility, and integrity. You don't pick these things up from books—they come from family, schools, churches, and community. I'm not the best judge of which of those qualities I have or to what degree, but much of the credit (or blame) for developing them goes to my adolescent years in the Sierra foothills.

The little town of Murphys calls itself the "Queen of the Sierra." It was a popular mining camp during the California gold rush. Thousands panned the Calaveras River and Murphys Creek for telltale yellow flakes. Irish immigrant brothers John and Daniel Murphy struck it rich, then made another fortune selling supplies to other prospectors. By the Civil War, the gold was mostly gone, and farmers, winemakers, and tourists gradually moved in. Mark Twain set his 1865 story "The Celebrated Jumping Frog of Calaveras County" eight miles down the road in the tiny Angels Camp, which still holds a frog-jumping contest every May.

Mom's mother, Mildred Roberts, deeded my parents half of her two-acre lot on Sheep Ranch Road, a few hundred yards north of downtown Murphys. Mom wanted a log cabin, and Dad was determined to build it with my help. Although *cabin* conjures up Daniel Boone and Abe Lincoln, ours was a prefab kit. Abe would not have been impressed. Dad hired a local contractor to level the rocky ground and pour a concrete slab foundation. A flatbed trailer brought a huge bundle of notched logs, insulation, windows, and roofing materials, along with step-by-step assembly instructions.

We drove up on Friday nights and slept at Grandma Mildred's—she had moved up there full time after her husband's death that spring—and headed home to South San Francisco on Sunday evenings. It was two and a half hours on the road each way. Dad didn't dwell on the meat business but was clearly happier than he had been a few months earlier. He wasn't much for heart-to-heart conversation, and neither was I. We chatted mostly about sports. It was a great year for the Giants; Willie McCovey hit forty-five home runs and almost made the playoffs, so there was a lot to discuss.

Our job was to hook cables to foundation rings, thread them through holes in the timbers, and cinch them at the roofline before placing roof supports. It would have been a doable undertaking for a couple of handymen. For a paunchy man and his fourteen-year-old son, it seemed a mission doomed from the get-go, but Dad was determined.

Dad was also stronger than he looked and surprisingly unfazed by the difficulty of forcing recalcitrant timbers into place and dealing with rain, mosquitoes, ants, and flies. The experience gave me a newfound appreciation for my father, whom I had dismissed as a typical suburban dad better suited to low-exertion activities like pushing a lawnmower or taking out the trash.

I wasn't thrilled about leaving the town I had known for what I considered the boonies. Mom and Dad gave me a BB gun at Christmas to mollify me, going on and on about how much fun I would have shooting at squirrels in the Sierra backwoods. On our weekend work trips, I woke early on Saturdays, hoping to take the weapon out in the sparse forest behind the house. Unfortunately, Dad got up earlier and wanted to get right to work. He insisted I labor for five or six hours, cleaning up the worksite, picking up wood scraps and nails, sweeping up, and keeping the job site neat. He didn't listen to my crybaby whining. If I did anything wrong, I had to do it again. It took us more than a year to finish the cabin. Looking back, I appreciate that he stuck to it. I credit that experience with later imbuing in me a love for work. I learned that few things are more satisfying than seeing a task through to the end and enjoying the fruits of my labor.

The log cabin project caught the attention of townspeople, who slowed to see what the strangers from San Francisco were up to. An old man in a pickup truck introduced himself as Burt Winslow. He lived four miles up the road on Shaw Ranch, a hilly spread where cattle grazed. Mr. Winslow became a regular visitor. We learned that he was a retired auditor and that his wife, Theolda, had recently died. "It gets lonely," he said.

Mr. Winslow said I could fish his trout stream whenever. One day, a friend and I wandered up to his home. It was an old farmhouse of hand-hewn square logs sealed with rope and white cement. It struck me as a real log house, not a lumberyard knockoff. Its scarred stone floors looked straight out of Pompeii, and the huge fireplace could warm a ballroom. An artesian spring flowed into a cement swimming pool. It was the first time I had ever seen a private pool. I imagined what it would be like to live there. Not long after that, Mr. Winslow brought us a basket of apples and pears. I overheard him and Dad talking. "I'm getting on," he said. "I can't keep up that place forever." He encouraged Dad to consider buying the ranch. "It would be good for your family," he said.

I could hardly hold my excitement. That night, I begged Dad to do it. He smiled and shook his head, as though I didn't understand the reality of life. A few weeks later, I brought up the subject again and got the same response. I was quietly furious. How could he ignore such an opportunity? I reasoned that it could only be due to a sad lack of ambition. He feared risk. I vowed not to be like that when I grew up. Only later did it dawn on me that Dad wasn't being timid; he was being an adult. He could no more afford that ranch than I could buy the Mark Hopkins Hotel.

Dad's reluctance to consider Mr. Winslow's offer made me aware of how much I differed from my dad in temperament and outlook. Having spent my early years in safe, comfortable surroundings, I had never personally experienced failure—at least in anything that really mattered to me. Sure, I had seen failure from afar, through the window of a truck in the bowels of San Francisco, but I hadn't felt the pangs of hunger or experienced the shame and anxiety of sleeping on the street and begging strangers for money.

Granted, my father never experienced those things firsthand, but he had witnessed widespread destitution and seen people he knew struggle. He considered financial security an illusion—a bubble that could burst at any moment. No paycheck, business venture, or savings account could be fully trusted, having seen too many families lose everything overnight. His generation lived with a constant undercurrent of anxiety, learning to get by with little, avoid debt, and always prepare for the worst.

I came of age in the prosperous 1950s and 1960s, when postwar optimism flourished, and the "good life" seemed achievable and inevitable. It was an era of new cars, suburban homes, and stable jobs—where economic growth and material success were taken for granted, leaving me to assume that the abundance surrounding us was permanent and secure. Where my father saw uncertainty lurking beneath every opportunity, I saw endless possibilities. This gave me a much higher tolerance for risk—perhaps even a conviction that opportunity was always there for the taking if you had the guts to go for it.

Dad got a management position at Middleton's Mark Twain Center, a furniture, appliance, hardware, and gift emporium in Angels Camp. The quiet predictability of small-town retail suited him. He became a community leader and a trustee of Mark Twain St. Joseph's Hospital. Mom worked as a nurse practitioner and did outreach for shut-ins.

School was a culture shock. I didn't know this kind of small-town world existed other than on TV. At El Camino, I had enjoyed anonymity, one of twenty-two hundred lookalike teens. Bret Harte High, in Angels Camp, had one hundred students. I felt exposed, naked, and out of place, with my San Francisco accent and hip suburban clothes. What was I doing there? I silently mocked their hokey rituals and obsession with Friday night football.

Gradually, I came around. Once I immersed myself in the local rhythms, I found meaning in experiences I had never imagined enjoying. As I got to know my schoolmates better, rural Calaveras County began to feel like home. Before long, I was hiking the pine forests like an American Indian scout and fishing hidden lakes with boys who had been doing those things all their lives. I had stepped out of *My Three Sons* into an old Andy Hardy movie—and loved it.

Friday, January 2, 1970, was my sixteenth birthday. I got to the DMV early. Uncle Nick had kept up with me from afar, sometimes driving down from the city to visit Dad. A car buff, he helped me scour newspapers for a cheap used vehicle, and we found a 1965 black Volkswagen Beetle with an eight-track stereo. He persuaded Dad to buy it.

With new friends, I cruised the back roads, chugging Coors like sailors on leave. When a Calaveras County Sheriff's deputy stopped us, we got a safe driving lecture and instructions to go home. What might be considered delinquent behavior today, especially in urban or suburban areas, was only normal teenage fun back then—barely worth a slap on the wrist in those simpler times.

As I drove two friends from a Friday night football game that autumn, events took a more serious turn. The lightweight Beetle clipped a boulder on a dark mountain road, flipped, and skidded on its side. No one was hurt, but I knew it looked bad: teenagers, beer, wrecked car. It was hard to see a good outcome. We searched the dark car floor for empty cans and threw them toward a ditch. Our aim was pitiful. The headlight of an approaching car revealed a dozen beer containers lying in the road. A blue light flashed.

I recognized the officer, and he knew me. The jig was up. After a long pause, he spoke. "Let's get this mess cleaned up, Bobby." The four of us righted the little car. Asphalt had sanded one side down to bare metal, but it started. I dropped my friends off and headed home to face the music. Dad was sleeping. I woke him to deliver the news before he found the damage in the morning light. He listened to my self-serving explanation, opened the front door, turned on the porch light, and stared at the bare metal. Finally, he turned and said, "You woke me for that?" Then he went back to bed and never mentioned it again.

I was relieved by his reaction but admittedly a little unsettled that he could be so blasé that I had narrowly avoided disaster. I expected anger, fear, or even concern. His indifference was unsettling. Was I being nudged out of the cozy family nest? Was I becoming independent, or was I already there?

The line between independence and rebelliousness is a tough one to straddle in adolescence. I liked security more than I would admit, but I also craved freedom. I took comfort in being part of the Campana clan, but I wanted my own identity. I was probably not that easy to be around when my rebellious streak surfaced.

Grandma Mildred was a focus of my resentment and the target of my occasionally obnoxious behavior. I considered her rigid, self-righteous, and an all-around pain. She had silver hair with a blue tint and wore cashmere sweaters with little clips to keep them on her shoulders. In my eyes, she was a steely eyed authoritarian, always telling me what to do. When she was anywhere near—which was almost always—I felt under siege. After three years in Murphys, I was at my breaking point. One hot autumn day, the Jeep I bought to replace the wounded Volkswagen broke down at the bottom of a hill three miles from home. As I stumbled, exhausted and sweaty, into the house, she glared at me. "I told you never to come in the house without firewood," she said. "Go back and do what you're supposed to do." Not bothering to point out that it was seventy degrees, I went to the woodpile.

Seething, I decided to show her what country life was really like. Once the Jeep was back in the driveway, I suggested we go for a ride. No doubt she was surprised by my sudden kindness. The trip wasn't what she expected. I showed her how the Jeep could bounce over the rockiest ground, turn on a dime, and tear through the deepest puddles without slowing down. She hung on to the grab bars like she was on the Big Dipper at Playland Park. She didn't say a word. When we walked into the house, Mom was standing in the living room. She stared at her mother, whose face was the color of Murphys Creek sediment except for two white, glasses-shaped orbs around her eyes. She looked like an owl. Mom glared at me. "What have you done?" I didn't try to answer. I knew I would be in the doghouse for weeks.

On several occasions, I drove my friends to concerts at The Fillmore, one of San Francisco's hottest music venues. We saw Cream, Frank Zappa, Carlos Santana, and Eric Clapton. We went to free Sunday afternoon concerts in Golden Gate Park, near Haight-Ashbury, where the counterculture movement was still going strong. Dazed hippies smoked marijuana and took psychedelics and other drugs. They shared weed with us. I also tried other drugs before realizing that my life was going in the wrong direction. Then I stopped. There wasn't one big event that forced me to change course, but rather a growing sense that I was headed toward trouble. I noticed how some of the people I hung out with were getting deeper into things I wasn't ready for—legal run-ins, overdoses, or just drifting aimlessly. They weren't going anywhere, and I didn't want to end up like that. The fun was wearing thin. At some point, I realized I wasn't chasing freedom—I was avoiding responsibility. That recognition scared me more than any drug, and it planted the seed for a deeper desire to straighten out before it was too late.

A turning point was a speech by Wilson C. Riles, a pioneering educator. He came to Murphys to formally close the state's last one-room schoolhouse, a structure built before the gold rush. Riles was California's superintendent of public instruction, the first Black person to hold a statewide office. In soft tones, he remarked on the wholesomeness of our small town and how our sort of upbringing was fading away. The world was changing, he said, but as we went through life, he hoped we would recall the unique grounding we had and the strong moral fiber we developed. He expressed confidence that, when confronting tough decisions, we would make the right ones. "You will be able to say, 'It's the Murphys in me.'" Dr. Riles repeated that phrase over and over throughout his speech. "You can't go home," he said finally, "but you can carry home with you."

Why do so many messages fail to stick, while others penetrate the soul? I have no idea, but Dr. Riles's words landed firmly in the latter category. They planted a deep sense of responsibility in me, a belief that who I was and where I came from mattered—and that my upbringing carried obligations beyond myself. His insistence that "you can carry home with you" gave me a lasting compass, shaping how I approached decisions, relationships, and even setbacks. I began to see integrity not just as an abstract ideal but as something grounded in the values of Murphys: community, honesty, and doing what's right, even when it's hard. Somehow, I knew that success wasn't just about what I achieved—it was about staying true to the moral fiber he spoke of, trusting that the principles I'd absorbed growing up would guide me through the most challenging moments of my life. Sometimes I still say to myself, "It's the Murphys in me."

I graduated from Bret Harte Union High School in Angels Camp, California, in June 1972. I had no idea what I wanted to do. I enrolled at Columbia Junior College in nearby Sonora but couldn't wrap my head around academia. In fact, I hated it. It wasn't that I rejected education altogether; I simply couldn't see the point unless I was aiming for a career that required professional credentials, like medicine or law. The things that mattered to me were tangible—hunting and fishing in the Sierras, working with my hands, and driving cars. Those activities felt real, offering skills and experiences I could hold on to, unlike the abstract lectures and theories professors droned on about. Even back then, college seemed more ideological than practical, a trend I believe has only worsened and contributed to many of the problems we see in the United States today—but I'll get into that later in this book. At eighteen, I was restless, eager to move on and dive into life, convinced that the real world had more to teach me than any classroom ever could. I wanted to get going, get out there, and live. But how? Doing what? With the Vietnam War still ongoing, I feared the draft. A couple of schoolmates went to Southeast Asia and came home in coffins. I got lucky. My number in the draft lottery was so high I knew I wouldn't have to go.

My first job was working for the federal government. I swept floors at the Murphys post office for $35 a week. It was a better gig than it sounds. Everyone in town went there daily to get their mail. I heard local gossip, met new people, and learned of job openings. Fred Kett, a local land surveyor, approached me while I was sweeping. His company had just won a contract to map a US Forest Service road in the Sierras. He was looking for people to join his crew, no surveying experience necessary. "I can use a young man like you," he said.

I was a chainman, following surveyors through the forest, staking out paths for bulldozers to follow. We hacked our way through virgin forests. Being outdoors was refreshing but vaguely sad, because I knew those towering trees would soon fall victim to soulless machines. Surveying helped me find new areas to hike and camp. I discovered chained Forest Service roads that few knew about. My official key would unlock them. Nobody knew we were there.

A few months into the job, a friend of a colleague was down from Sacramento. I offered to show him some of the natural wonders I had discovered. Later, I learned he had no experience on narrow, curvy mountain roads. He lost control, and his pickup tumbled a hundred yards down the side of a ravine. A tree peeled the roof like a can opener, and a sharp edge sliced through a tendon in my hand.

Semiconscious, I somehow had the presence of mind to wrap my arm with a shirt and hold it above my head. Two friends in the car behind raced me to the hospital. Fortunately, the emergency room physician knew that a San Francisco orthopedic surgeon had a vacation cabin nearby and called him in to do the repairs. A follow-up operation allowed me to move my fingers. I couldn't work for more than a month, but a $12,000 insurance settlement more than made up for the lost wages.

Fred Kett lost the Forest Service contract to a bigger out-of-town company, but the new one kept our team on because we knew the territory. I got a raise, plus $60 a day for food and lodging. My colleagues and I figured out we could double our take-home by camping and cooking our own food. Over the next year, I saved $7,000. With that and the insurance payout in the bank, I felt rich for the first time in my life.

I lay in my tent late at night, reading by lantern light and listening to a radio I brought from home. It was hard to get a clear signal in the Sierras, but two stations came in strong. One featured a Bible-thumper named Garner Ted Armstrong, who read Scripture, put world events in religious perspective, and urged listeners to follow the teachings of the Worldwide Church of God. I got a kick out of listening to him. Other nights, I favored the gravelly voice and eerie howl of Wolfman Jack, who blasted rock music from a powerful transmitter just over the border in Mexico. As the soulful sounds of Don McLean, Elton John, and Bill Withers filled my tent, I fantasized about what I would do with my money.

"A Porsche? Wouldn't it be wiser to go back to college?" Dad's tone was annoyingly reasonable. There was no use arguing. As far as I was concerned, his Depression-era ideas were hopelessly out of sync with the modern world. In the California of the 1970s, a car was your identity, and I knew what I wanted my identity to be: confident, adventurous, and effortlessly cool. In my mind, I was the image of freedom, success, and sophistication—someone who lived on his terms, unburdened by convention.

I found a silver 1968 911L, owned by a guy in the Bay Area who made a lot of money doing hair plugs for balding men. I paid $8,000 cash, less than half my bank balance. No guys my age had such a car, especially one that was fully paid for. I raced it around the Calaveras County back roads. At one point, I spun out and wrecked a rear tail panel and had to get it fixed, but that didn't slow me down. Years later, I learned that the 1968 911L was the rarest Porsche ever made. It was a special model designed to pass the stringent California smog test. It replaced the fuel injection system with six one-barrel carburetors that could be adjusted to balance the fuel-air mixture. Today, the cheapest one you can find is $290,000.

Sometimes I hung out at the bar of the historic Murphys Hotel, where locals and tourists congregated. It was the only place in town that had live music. A dark-haired young woman with a south-western accent conversed with a girl I knew from high school. I edged my way in. Her name was Joyce. Over drinks, she told me that she had moved to Murphys from Dallas right out of high school to live with her boyfriend on his brother's three-thousand-acre cattle ranch. They got married, but ranching life didn't appeal to her, and they had since divorced. With no place to live or source of income, she was headed back to Texas. I saw her again the next night. We seemed to hit it off. She gave me her parents' Dallas phone number, and I called her half a dozen times over the next month. I suggested driving down to see her. I wasn't certain how she felt, but my charm enticed her to say yes. It was my first long road trip in the Porsche— or in any vehicle.

After driving twenty-one hours straight, I only had about two hundred twenty miles to go to reach Dallas, but I had to stop, sleep, and shower. I got a room at a rundown hotel in the small town of Sweetwater, Texas, just west of Abilene. The next morning, I thought I had wandered onto the set of *The Last Picture Show*, where everyone lived bleak lives in a dying Western town. *If this was what Texas was all about*, I thought, *I have no need for it*. I almost turned around and headed back to the Sierras. But the thought of Joyce waiting in Dallas with open arms made me press on. Any fantasies I had about a deep romance met cold reality. She had other plans: American Airlines had accepted her as a flight attendant and would transfer her to Chicago after training. A few months later, I visited her in the Windy City, where she lived in a tiny flat with four colleagues near the Playboy Mansion. It was clear that she had a new life, and I was not part of it. That didn't bother me too much because I, too, had other plans.

## Entrepreneurial Life Lessons

- Hard skills aren't enough to build a strong business; you also need vision, resilience, and adaptability and core values like gratitude, humility, and integrity.

- While some fear uncertainty, entrepreneurs see endless possibilities and are willing to take the necessary risks.

- Understanding your risk tolerance begins with understanding yourself.

# 3

# Pan Am

## Farewell Comfort Zone

The entrepreneurial drive may start at home, but it flourishes on the road. Travel broadens perspectives, challenges assumptions, and sparks creativity. Stepping into unfamiliar cultures pushes you out of your comfort zone, forcing you to adapt, problem-solve, and see opportunities where others might not. It teaches you resilience; navigating language barriers, unfamiliar customs, and unexpected setbacks mirrors the uncertainty of running a business.

For me, travel has been an endless source of inspiration, offering fresh insights on how people work, live, and consume—lessons I've applied to business ventures in ways I never could have predicted from behind a desk. No matter how different people seem on the surface, they share fundamental needs—connection, trust, and meaning—values that are as essential in business as they are in life.

When I set off around the world at age twenty-one, I didn't realize how formative it would be or how it would shape the course of my life and career. But it planted a seed of curiosity and wanderlust that has guided many of my choices since.

Marie and Victor Marchette were an older couple who lived near my parents on Sheepranch Road. She worked at the post office, and he was a retired truck driver. In high school, I earned a few dollars a week feeding their four dozen hogs. Their grandsons, Steve and Bruce, visited them every summer. We were about the same age, and they didn't know anybody up there, so we soon became a team. I introduced them to little-known back trails and fishing spots. They showed me pictures and told me stories of expat life in Iran, France, and Indonesia, where their dad was a senior executive with the giant French American oil services company Schlumberger. They regaled me on the exploits of their uncle, a medical scientist in Hawaii who prowled Malaysian jungles collecting monkey blood samples. These were ways of life I could scarcely imagine.

In the late summer of 1974, Steve, Bruce, and I hiked the hilly South Grove Trail in Calaveras Big Trees State Park, fifteen miles up the road from Murphys. We followed the Stanislaus River, the giant sequoias that awed early settlers soaring overhead. It was quieter at that time of year, but they still murmured in the background.

Steve, then a junior at the University of Santa Clara, reminisced about backpacking with his brother through Southeast Asia and India two years earlier. They had set out from their parents' home in Jakarta and joined thousands of other adolescent wanderers on the so-called hippie trail through Indonesia, Malaysia, India, the Himalayas, and the Middle East. They toyed with doing it again in 1975. It might be their last chance, as their dad would be transferred back to Paris. Pan Am sold a $2,300 around-the-world ticket that let you board a westbound 747 in California, get off at any stop, stay as long as you wanted, and hop on an ongoing flight. "Why don't you come along?" Steve said. I smiled, not sure whether his suggestion was an actual proposal or just idle musing. At his grandparents' house a couple of days later, I brought it up. "Were you serious about my tagging along in Asia?" He had a goofy smile. "Of course," he said.

The idea seemed fanciful, impractical, quixotic. What business did I, a Sierra chainman with no college education, have traveling halfway around the world with world-wise university kids? I knew little about anything outside Northern California. A few days in Texas and Chicago were one thing; going halfway around the world for months was another story. What about my job? How could I afford the airfare, let alone six months' worth of food, lodging, and incidentals? How could I explain it to my dad, who I suspected thought of me as borderline profligate for buying the Porsche? Still, the prospect excited me as I lay in my little Sierra tent over the next few weeks, listening to owls, bubbling streams, and the faraway howls of Wolfman Jack.

I bounced the idea off friends and family. One of my sisters suggested I read James Michener's popular 1971 novel *The Drifters*, which followed six enlightenment-seeking young wanderers through Europe and Africa. I wasn't much for literature, but I checked it out and read it in my tent. The book touched something in me the same way Dr. Riles's speech had. It stirred an unfamiliar hunger, a desire to be part of something bigger than my comfortable and predictable existence in the Sierra foothills. It was a feeling that would come to consume my thoughts, alter my perspective, drive business decisions, and shape my family's lives.

The characters, all about my age, left conventional paths to seek purpose and connection in exotic locales like Spain, Morocco, and Mozambique. They thrived on the freedom that came with travel.

Their journeys captured the spirit of the open road and celebrated the personal liberation that came with wandering without constraints. They reveled in a lifestyle free of routine, where societal expectations dissolved. I didn't consider myself disillusioned, but I shared their determination. After finishing the book, the question in my mind was no longer whether I wanted to go with the Marchettes; it was about how I would make it happen.

Fifteen thousand dollars—that's how much I figured I would need. It wouldn't be easy to get, but doable. I still had insurance money from the accident. I could also sell my car—not something I relished doing, but it was a sacrifice I was prepared to make. I phoned Steve and told him to count me in.

We left in April 1975. I tucked $4,000 of American Express traveler's checks in a money belt and flew to Los Angeles, where Steve, his girlfriend, Ann, and his brother, Bruce, met me at LAX. We boarded a 747 to Honolulu. After two nights with his monkey-hunting uncle, we left for Tokyo. We would only be there for twelve hours between connections, and could camp in the terminal, but I wanted to see Ginza, Japan's famous shopping, dining, and enter-tainment district. Steve said it was like an upscale version of New York's increasingly seedy Times Square. By the time we got through customs at the aging Haneda Airport, it was close to midnight. Since Tokyo subways shut down for overnight maintenance, we pooled our money to cab it downtown. Ginza was almost deserted at 1 a.m. Unlocked bikes were neatly lined up along Chuo-dori Street. Steve and I joked that those bikes wouldn't have lasted ten minutes in San Francisco's Union Square. I watched a man patiently wait for a walk signal, though there wasn't a car in sight.

Mr. Marchette had said we could stay at their house in Jakarta for a day or so before hitting the trail. He and his wife were out of town, but their driver would meet us at the airport. Our afternoon flight from Tokyo, with a change in Hong Kong, got us to Jakarta in fifteen hours. The Marchettes lived in Menteng, near embassies and government offices. It was a leafy neighborhood, with big Western-style homes built before the First World War. Security seemed tight; high concrete walls with metal spikes surrounded the house. A guard eyed us but didn't say anything as we got out of the car. A servant in a short-sleeved shirt and sandals showed me to an airy room on the second floor with a ceiling fan and mosquito netting over the bed. He nodded politely, told me to call him if I needed anything, and slipped away. It reminded me of the old Audie Murphy movie *The Quiet American*, set in 1950s Saigon. A different servant served us some kind of chicken with peanut sauce in a veranda garden with bougainvillea and palms. I was impressed; Schlumberger treated its executives well.

The next day, Steve, Ann, Bruce, and I rode an elevator to the top of the famous Monas Tower monument. We lunched like affluent expats in the Old Town district and listened to a jazz band at the Hotel Indonesia. It was a rarefied life, giving me a fleeting peek into a world far removed from anything I'd known. The next day, the driver dropped us off at a bus station and bid us farewell as we journeyed into a radically different world.

Steve led; I had no clue where we were going. We squeezed onto a crowded, ancient bus, sliding around on the hard plastic bench seats whenever the driver hit the brakes. Open windows provided the only ventilation in the ninety-degree heat. Every hour or so, the bus pulled up next to a food stall with rudimentary squat toilets out back—usually just a ceramic or concrete basin set into the ground, with no flush mechanism. A small bucket of water and a ladle sat nearby for manual flushing and washing.

In Yogyakarta, a medium-sized city, we paid $2 each to sleep on wooden beds covered with mosquito nets and thin woven mats.

My Sierra tent was the Ritz in comparison. Even with a sleeping bag on top, I woke up with stiff joints. But who was complaining? The experience more than made up for it.

The next day was all about walking, soaking in history, and reveling in the exotic culture. We explored Borobudur, a massive Buddhist temple with intricate stone carvings, and climbed to the top to take in the view. We toured Prambanan, a Hindu temple with tall spires. I welcomed the calm after bustling Jakarta.

Walking would be our main mode of transportation over the next three weeks. Steve navigated on impulse, often following recommendations from other backpackers we met on the roads or in villages. We slept where we could find cheap or free accommodations—guesthouses, temple courtyards, or train stations. We camped outdoors on beaches or in parks. Kind locals occasionally let us sleep in storage huts, barns, or rice shelters. We lived on *nasi goreng* (fried rice) or *satay* (skewered chicken, beef, lamb, or goat, usually seasoned with turmeric and coriander). We bought them at ubiquitous local street stalls—*warungs*—for twenty cents a plate.

Few rural people had cars; most rode bicycles or scooters along narrow dirt roads. I saw no offices or factories. People harvested rice; tended water buffalo, goats, and ducks; and ran one-person shops selling dried fish and woven baskets. I couldn't help but wonder: Where did they get money for things they couldn't make themselves—say, fuel and medicine? It was an economy without a visible structure, where the boundary between personal labor and livelihood blurred completely.

Locals were as fascinated by us as we were by them. Younger people, especially, seemed well versed in American culture—Coca-Cola and Marlboro, Hollywood stars, and rock bands like the Beatles or Jimi Hendrix. They asked us in Malay, mixed with broken English, about life in the United States, why we would leave our comfortable lives to travel around with little money. It was hard to explain.

Malay, or some variant of it, was pretty much the *lingua franca*. The Marchettes knew a little. As we trooped along a dirt road in central Java, Steve called out to a bamboo-hatted farmer hoeing something that looked like tobacco. The man smiled. Half his teeth were missing. I gathered from a brief conversation that the man's family had worked the land for ten generations, but he feared that his son and two daughters would move to the city. He had that in common with American farmers.

On an otherwise deserted road in Bali, we traded stories with a bearded American going the other way. He urged us to visit a quaint seaside village he had just left. "It's paradise," he said. It was a two- or three-mile walk. At the only restaurant, I was delighted to see a few bottles of Coke in a glass-front cooler. They turned out to be warm, but I was happy for any taste of home. That night, elders sat around a campfire near the restaurant, conversing in a rhythmic dialect we could not understand. They ignored us. A dollar bought four bowls of nasi goreng. We negotiated an overnight stay in a small hut near a bamboo latrine. In the morning, we watched large frigatebirds soar along the water's edge like ancient pterodactyls and decided the stranger was right about paradise.

Experiences like that invariably alter your perspective on life. Anthony Bourdain, a fellow restaurateur, got it exactly right in his book *No Reservations: Around the World on an Empty Stomach*. "Travel isn't always pretty," he wrote. "It isn't always comfortable. Sometimes it hurts, it even breaks your heart. But that's okay. The journey changes you; it should change you."

Five weeks in urban and rural Southeast Asia upended my assumption that the lifestyle I had grown up with was the natural state of human existence. There were clearly many other ways to live happily—some of them harsh but marked by a resilience I couldn't help but admire. At the same time, I gained a new appreciation for what Americans, most of them immigrants, had achieved: a standard of living that once only kings enjoyed, one that continued to draw millions to its doors. What lessons could I take from these contrasting worlds? I had no answer, but merely asking the question suggested that I was on an interesting journey.

For travelers on the 1975 hippie trail, India was the logical next stop. It was a magnet for those seeking spiritual guidance. Indian guru Maharishi Mahesh Yogi drew the Beatles, the Beach Boys, and Mia Farrow with something called *transcendental meditation*. I was curious about these strange practices.

Steve's dad telegraphed that we could decamp at a colleague's house in a New Delhi neighborhood called Chanakyapuri. It was another lush, green enclave with the luxurious homes of foreign diplomats and rich expats. Once again, I was among society's sheltered elite.

But that wasn't the India I wanted to see. A half-hour taxi ride took us to Chandni Chowk, in Old Delhi. The streets were chaotic, filled with rickshaws, carts, and cows. I could hardly walk without bumping into someone. Vendors pushed overflowing carts. Some sold salty snacks called *chaat*, made with fried dough, potatoes, chickpeas, yogurt, and chutney. Others sold cooking utensils, underwear, or small toys. Scents of turmeric, incense, and diesel fuel filled my nostrils. At night, the crowds vanished, replaced by solitary wanderers, the so-called untouchables, carrying sticks to start fires and cook whatever food they could find. Purplish smoke hovered over everything. I had seen poverty in rural Indonesia, but Delhi was different: harsher and grimmer but also more animated. I wondered what was worse.

The next day, we visited popular tourist sites like the Red Fort, Jama Masjid, India Gate, Qutub Minar, and Humayun's Tomb. The old Mughal architecture exuded history. The political air was heavy; armed police and soldiers were out in force. I felt uneasy for the first time on our long journey. Apparently, Prime Minister Indira Gandhi had declared a state of emergency, suspended civil liberties, and cracked down on political opposition. Censors blacked out newspaper and magazine articles. We walked and talked softly, careful not to attract attention, fearful that a slip of the tongue might get us in trouble.

We planned to take a train north to Kashmir, where the weather would be cooler and the crowds less intense. Steve suggested going first to Varanasi, about 450 miles southeast. "You can't really understand India until you've been there," he said. Varanasi was one of the holiest cities in Hinduism. It was famous for its *ghats* along the Ganges River, where religious pilgrims performed rituals and ceremonies.

We traveled fifteen hours in a second-class compartment of an overnight express, sleeping as best we could on hard seats.

At Manikarnika Ghat, English-speaking tourist guides clustered around the steps leading down to the water, where cremations took place. Steve paid a lean man in sandals ten rupees—about a dollar—to walk with us and explain what we would see. The smoky incense and the sound of chanting filled the air. On the riverbank, men placed a body wrapped in white sheets on a stack of logs. The family tossed on ghee and sandalwood. The eldest son said prayers as flames consumed the corpse. The acrid smell of burning flesh seared my nostrils; I tried not to think about what I was breathing. Later, we went out on a little boat and watched the city come alive.

Back in Delhi, we boarded a packed train to northern India. Mughal emperors summered there from the early 1500s to the mid-1800s. India, Pakistan, and China had jockeyed for control since India's partition in 1947. In the summer capital of Srinagar, we watched hundreds of Muslims protest something; we weren't sure what. A man chanted into a megaphone. Hundreds of glassy-eyed protesters shuffled like zombies, chanting something in monotone. They showed no emotion. It was like *The Walking Dead*. My skin crawled. We walked away as fast as we could.

In Srinagar, we rented a tiny houseboat cabin on Dal Lake, a famously picturesque body of water near the city center, and watched the sun rise over the Himalayas. We'd heard it was an almost mystical experience but hadn't expected the squadron of floating vendors that drifted up before we finished breakfast. Five men leaped, uninvited, onto our moored boat with bags of produce, spices, fabric, and papier-mâché crafts. A rug merchant nagged me onto his barge, piled so high with carpets I worried it might tip over. He insisted that I feel each one. Despite their seemingly fluent English, none of our visitors understood the word *no*.

Our next destination, Nepal, was seven hundred fifty miles by air from Srinagar, twice that by road. With no direct flights available, we voted to take a bus to the Nepal border and another to the country's capital city of Kathmandu. We figured it would take us a couple of days. We traveled for three, often over narrow mountain roads with no guardrails that made me close my eyes and hold my breath.

We rented a hut in the touristy Thamel district. Backpackers jammed the narrow streets and little shops. The hostel manager said wild monkeys liked to steal shiny objects and warned us to keep shutters latched. The occupant of an adjacent room apparently didn't listen; a simian snatched an Instamatic camera from a dresser, carried it to the top of a tree, and smashed it on a rock below. His compatriots scrambled down to pick at the pieces.

Steve and I bought cheap fishing poles at a shop and asked the owner where we could use them. He pointed to a map dotted with ponds. We picked one at random, a half mile away. It was more secluded than we expected, surrounded by dense vegetation and a beautifully landscaped garden. We congratulated ourselves on our good fortune but caught nothing, so we ditched the poles and walked back to the hut. The manager gave us a look when we told her about our fishing adventure. The pond, she said, was the private preserve of the king and strictly off-limits to nonroyals. How had we slipped past the armed soldiers? They jailed trespassers. We laughed, but the next day, I shuddered at our narrow escape.

Pan Am didn't fly from Kathmandu to New Delhi, so it routed us on Air India to the capital, where we caught a Pan Am 747 to Lebanon. It should have been a routine flight. Beirut was a world-class, cosmopolitan city, sometimes called the Paris of the Middle East. We looked forward to a couple of days strolling along the Corniche by the Mediterranean and experiencing the vibrant bars, nightclubs, and jazz venues.

Thanks to Indian censors, we didn't know civil war was well underway there. When the plane left New Delhi, the pilot told us the unpleasant truth: We were bound for a war zone. At Beirut International, the plane stopped five hundred yards from the terminal. A flight attendant instructed us to walk the rest of the way. Soldiers lined the route. Small-arms fire echoed in the distance. I felt rubble under my feet and saw bullet holes in the terminal's concrete walls. An airline agent steered us into a small room and gave us a choice: Stay in Beirut at our own risk or take the next flight to Paris. We just wanted to get the hell out. After some tense hours, we were back in the air.

On arrival at the new Charles de Gaulle Airport, I felt as if a cloud had lifted. The Marchettes' dad had transferred to Paris and lived in a spacious apartment with a view of the Eiffel Tower. I gazed over old slate rooftops and brick chimneys. Mr. Marchette said I could stay as long as I wanted. I got the impression that Steve and Bruce wanted to spend some private time with their parents, and I understood. I, too, was homesick for family and friends, so I decided to take the next Pan Am flight across the Atlantic.

After five months on the road together, I said goodbye to my travel companions, who now seemed like family, and boarded a flight to New York. I had a day layover and wanted a glimpse of the Big Apple. I sat next to a young man on an elevated Manhattan-bound train. He wrapped his arms tightly around a brown paper package. Never shy about talking with strangers, I asked him about it. "It's my new boom box. I need to get it home without anybody seeing it." Thieves sometimes rushed onto cars as soon as the doors opened, grabbed what they could, and scooted off before the doors slid shut. "They will steal anything," he said, adding that you had to admire their timing and nerve. I wasn't so impressed. I spent one night at a cheap hotel near Times Square, walked around looking at peep-show marquees, and avoided eye contact with slick-looking guys passing out handbills. After a few hours, I couldn't wait to get the hell out of town. New York scared me more than anywhere I'd been. How could anyone live there?

Looking down at the busy Bayshore Freeway in front of San Francisco International, I felt like a different person than the one who left that same airport five months earlier. I saw the world through a new lens. I had seen the spectrum of human society. The intensity of Asian cities awed me. The adversity that third-world people experience daily shocked and humbled me. I had seen absolute poverty for the first time and couldn't forget it. People in the South Bronx were rich by comparison.

For the first time, I realized how lucky I was to be born in America. I thought of how my grandparents had arrived on these shores with little and prospered through hard work and persistence. Did I have that same grit in me? I owed it to them and to myself to find out.

## Entrepreneurial Life Lessons

- Growth comes from leaving your comfort zone and pushing boundaries.

- Achieving meaningful goals requires understanding your priorities and making sacrifices.

- True fulfillment begins with appreciating your circumstances and recognizing the value of what you already have.

# 4

# Hot Tubs

## Making Rookie Mistakes

**A**mbition and energy are fine qualities for any would-be entre-preneur, but charging blindly ahead can lead you down a rocky road. I learned that the hard way.

I was back where I had left off eight months earlier, but poorer. My bank account was empty, and I had no car, no source of income, and no plan. My parents were so happy to have me home that they weren't hassling me to pay rent or buy food. Still, I couldn't just sit there and do nothing.

At dinner, Dad asked the question I knew was coming: "What are your plans?" He said it lightly, but his eyes were serious. "Do you think you can get back on the survey team?"

I rolled my eyes. "That was a dead-end job," I said, a little too sharply. I was done with hourly work, selling my precious time for weekly paychecks. Describing my epiphany over the Bayshore

Freeway, I explained that I would strike out on my own and exploit the country's opportunities. I would start a business.

Dad said nothing, but I could sense the mood shift in the room. Mom left the table to check something in the kitchen. Kathleen and Laureen remembered they had homework to do. I fiddled with a fork as Dad looked at me with compassion and frustration. His voice took on the parental tone I remembered from building the log cabin. "I'm not sure you know what you are talking about," he said. Starting a business required an idea, a plan, and capital, he said, none of which I had.

I left the table angry. Even if what he said made sense, it only stiffened my resolve. My mind raced with business ideas: opening a gas station, starting a wilderness guide service, renting out boats to vacationers. None seemed bold or imaginative enough. Where did opportunity lie? I had no clue. I was in a rowboat without an oar, hoping to wash ashore somewhere magical.

In the meantime, I needed cash to buy a car, go to bars with friends, and have a life. Being a capitalist was harder than I thought. Dad didn't rub it in my face, but I imagined what he was thinking. Despite my earlier declaration not to work for a paycheck, I reluctantly rejoined the mountain survey crew to put cash in my pocket.

Jim Farrell, a high school friend who had moved to San Francisco, invited me to a hot tub party in Marin County in the summer of 1976. I had never heard of a *hot tub*. He said ex-hippies communed half naked in outdoor bathtubs, smoking dope and exorcising their inner demons. "It should be fun." I wasn't sure about that, but I had nothing better to do. I was up for anything. After traveling in Asia and India, I vowed to explore every cranny of life.

Marin, just north of San Francisco, across the Golden Gate Bridge, was a mecca for affluent professionals, artists, and countercultural figures seeking a blend of natural beauty, privacy, and progressive community living. Its picturesque landscapes, outdoor lifestyle, and proximity to the Bay Area attracted wealthy urbanites, including tech entrepreneurs, corporate executives, and creatives.

It was a three-hour drive on a Saturday afternoon. The party was at a house overlooking a woodsy valley. I met Jim in a little clearing, where a dozen Japanese and German cars were parked askew. A woman in a long paisley dress smooched Jim on the cheek and walked away, ignoring me. Sandal-wearers knotted about, sipping wine from glasses. Five or six people sat in a redwood vat about the diameter of a kiddie swimming pool. I wasn't sure which toes belonged to which body. I thought: *This is where Haight-Ashbury kids go after law school.* I felt out of place, a spectator at someone else's strange ritual. Driving home through the darkness, I couldn't help reflecting on what I had witnessed. The half-spiritual, half-self-indulgent, privileged life wasn't my thing, but those people were moving on with life, and I wasn't.

Barden Stevenot was a successful real estate developer who had bought the old Shaw Ranch that Burt Winslow tried to sell Dad. He was developing a vineyard, hoping to revive a local wine industry that flickered out in Prohibition. Before going abroad, I helped him string fence and lay irrigation pipe. "Come see me when you get back," he said. "I could use a young man like you."

I phoned him. He invited me to his office in Burt Winslow's old house. Forty years old, with smiling eyes and a droopy mustache, he might have fit in with the Marin crowd if he were twenty years younger. He perked up when I mentioned the hot tub party and pulled out a newspaper clipping about Pacific Gas and Electric selling off miles of old redwood pipeline in the mountains for next to nothing. "Do you think someone could make hot tubs from these things?"

I did some research. A *Sunset* magazine article suggested that hot tubs were the next big home accoutrement. A physical therapist at the hospital explained how whirlpools relaxed muscles and eased stress. I consulted a plumbing supply house, a swimming pool contractor, and the Sears catalog for ideas. A carpenter said he could make one out of redwood, but he thought water leaks might be an issue. I told Barden what I had learned, but his mind seemed elsewhere. I let the subject drop.

Meanwhile, I craved adventure. Surveying had improved my bank balance, but the project had inexplicably stalled. A laid-off colleague named Jack asked, "Want to go to South America?" I said, "Sure." Two weeks later, with $400 round-trip Pan Am tickets, we set off for Ecuador. The next five weeks are a blur of memories, almost a fever dream: bouncing through the rainforest in a rented Land Cruiser, canoeing down the Rio Napo as howler monkeys screamed and loinclothed hunters stared. In Quevedo, we befriended a Chiquita Bananas heiress who was there to dedicate a public swimming pool the company had financed. She invited us to sit with her and local officials at a ceremonial dinner. Later, I danced into the night with local girls as a mariachi band played, trumpets swaying back and forth with the music. In the end, the audience declared me King of Cabezon (I learned later, to my chagrin, that *cabezon* means "big-headed"). Jack and I wanted to take in the Galapagos Islands but had no money. Luckily, my backpack held the return ticket home.

Upon my return to Murphys, Barden called. "If I bought the redwood," he asked, "would you help my crew make hot tubs?" We would haul pipelines down from the mountains, craft the tubs in a vacant vineyard barn, and sell them to locals. He would pay me an hourly wage for work in the shop. Once the tubs were built, I had the option to buy them on credit and sell them for whatever retail markup I could get. I knew nothing about building hot tubs and had never sold anything, but what did I have to lose? On the eve of my twenty-third birthday, my hand shook with excitement as I signed an agreement and became an entrepreneur.

Barden's motivation for the project was unclear. He didn't need the money and had his hands full with the winery. Perhaps he saw it as an interesting little side project. Maybe he was giving back to the community by creating a new industry. Or maybe he aimed to help a struggling young man grab the first rung of success. Whatever the case, he was an inspiration, the polar opposite of my risk-avoidant father. He forged ahead, blazed new trails, confident he could handle what came and learn along the way. He was basically building a winery from scratch in an area that hadn't had a successful one in fifty years. He didn't know a thing about wine, as far as I could tell, but he didn't let that stop him. He had books all over his office about winemaking. He gathered all the information he could. He knew that Sierra frost could destroy a grape harvest overnight, but he was willing to take that risk. Going into the nascent hot tub business with a twenty-three-year-old business novice was also a risk. But he never wavered, honored his commitments, and patiently managed my quirks and lack of direction with kindness and support. That made a big impression on me.

My girlfriend suggested I team up with her brother, who worked part time at their father's construction company in Angels Camp. "He can use power tools," she said. Her brother and I had been high school classmates—friendly but not close. He was exactly as I remembered: slim, long sandy hair, sketchy whiskers, and a laid-back vibe. He wanted in. I readily agreed to a fifty-fifty partnership because I wanted someone to share the workload, brainstorm ideas, and have my back. In retrospect, it was one of the worst business judgments I ever made. Like teenage marriages, hasty business partnerships often lead to years of regret. Neither is easily nor inexpensively dissolved. It's a lesson I haven't forgotten.

My new partner was energetic and worked hard. We winched six-hundred-pound sections of redwood pipe onto a flatbed truck high above the Stanislaus River and trucked them down to Barden's barn. We cut them into three-foot sections, fashioned bottoms from new lumber, and sealed the cracks with rope and tar. We sprayed on varnish and attached white plastic pipes and an electric heater ordered from a plumbing supply house. Barden stopped by from time to time to offer moral support but otherwise left us alone.

After a month, the newly formed Vintage Hot Tubs company had five beautiful redwood creations ready to go. But where? I posted flyers at the Sierra Hills Market and put a small ad in the *Calaveras Enterprise*, hoping to attract vacation homeowners from the Bay Area. Silence. Hot tubs might be the new thing in Northern California, but Calaveras County hadn't gotten the word.

The stress made me cranky and difficult to be around. My girlfriend, my partner's sister, dumped me. I booked a solitary trip to New Zealand, hoping naively that travel would cure heartbreak. Besides, there was no point in sticking around to build more hot tubs only to watch them gather dust in the corner.

I returned from New Zealand with a newfound appreciation for fly fishing and a bold idea. We needed to be in a bigger, richer market more attuned to modern vibes. Modesto, an hour down Route 99, had much more potential. A city of 85,000, it sat at the edge of California's fertile Central Valley. Dairy, almond, and grape farms generated a lot of wealth. So did the enormous Gallo Winery. The town had plenty of young doctors, lawyers, and world-wise executives—the kind of affluent up-and-comers who read *Sunset* magazine and would surely latch on to the latest luxury craze. The little city was enjoying fifteen minutes of fame as the setting of George Lucas's massively successful movie *American Graffiti*. It was the place to be. My partner knew the city, having once sold waterbeds at a Modesto furniture store, so I ran the idea by him. "Sure," he said. "That might work." It was hardly a rousing cheer, but I suspected that was as much enthusiasm as I would get from him.

We rented a three-bedroom ranch house on Staci Lane in a new development east of town as our home and place of business. A two-car garage fronting the street served as a showroom. With the aid of a small ad in the *Modesto Bee*, we sold two tubs in the first month, which provided enough money to rent a tiny commercial space behind a coffee shop on McHenry Ave, a busy corridor lined with car dealerships and fast-food outlets.

We installed a working model out back so people could see it in action; we even kept the water warm at night, hoping people would try it out after closing. That would be unfathomable today due to health, safety, and insurance reasons, but it got us noticed. We often found pieces of clothing, orphaned shoes, and other personal items—some of which I can't mention—scattered about in the morning.

The showroom gave customers a glimpse, but the real sale happened once we planned everything on-site. People would walk into the showroom and look at the model. Sometimes they liked what they saw and gave us a deposit on the spot, but more often than not, they'd say, "We want to see how it would look at our house." I'd visit their home, and we'd figure out where it would go. We'd discuss details like positioning and interior design to help them visualize the final look.

Contrary to our expectations, few of our early customers were ex-hippies or affluent young professionals. Most were older folks seeking relief from rheumatism and other aches and pains. Families sometimes bought them as kid-size pools.

Before long, we were selling one or two custom-size hot tubs a week. I phoned the specs to Barden's crew, who built them to order. My partner and I drove to Murphys on Friday evenings, loaded them in a black Dodge van, and installed them the following week. We dug a hole half the tub's height, put a cement pad at the bottom, connected plumbing and electricity, and in many cases built a surrounding redwood deck. The total cost could approach $7,000, the sticker price of a Ford Thunderbird or entry-level BMW. Even after paying Barden, half of that was profit.

Collaborating with my partner revealed a side of him I found unappealing. He often approached the business lightly, treating it as a lark rather than a serious endeavor. He made immature jokes at inopportune moments. When we arrived at the home of one middle-aged couple to begin an installation, the husband, a lanky, weathered man named Lew, mowed the lawn wearing white high heels and a woman's yellow two-piece bathing suit. My partner looked at me and started to say something. I gave him a look. As we worked, he sang a little ditty: "Lew, Lew, what's wrong with you? What do you do? You're a strange one, blue." He repeated it, louder. I looked to see if Lew had heard. "Enough," I said. He rolled his eyes and smirked. I was beginning to wonder whether partnering with him was smart.

It was also clear that while he knew his way around equipment, my partner was painfully awkward around people. We called on an older couple interested in a hot tub for arthritis relief. They invited us into their small living room. As I engaged them in banter, he hunkered silently, shifting impatiently in his chair. He gave the impression that he was there only to get a deposit and get the hell out. Sensing rejection, I turned on the charm, nodding sympathetically as the couple described their aches and pains. I made them laugh and steered the conversation to a successful close.

Driving home, I suggested tactfully that I be the face of the business and that he stick to installation. I expected pushback, but he nodded in agreement. I decided that selling was my true calling. World travel had given me an air of sophistication and an easy manner that the average twenty-three-year-old lacked. I look back on that realization as a turning point in my life.

Hot tubs were hot. By 1978, doctors, lawyers, and executives embraced them, soaking to unwind after long days. Redwood spas were status symbols, along with tennis courts, swimming pools, and high-end outdoor kitchens. They conveyed wealth and sophistication. Modesto's Mediterranean climate gave them a year-round appeal—comforting on cool fall and winter evenings and refreshing on summer nights. Kids splashed around in them during the day.

In its first year, Vintage Hot Tubs sold and installed nearly one hundred units and grossed half a million dollars. My partner managed all installations with the help of hired freelance carpenters, plumbers, and electricians. My days were wholly devoted to fielding inquiries, measuring yards, ordering supplies, writing checks for ads, fuel, insurance, and a dozen other things.

In the mirror, I saw a successful entrepreneur destined for greatness. My grandfather would be impressed. But sometimes, it's too easy to mistake luck for smarts. My cocky confidence soon collapsed. Two California state sales tax investigators showed up one morning, demanding to see our files. After a painful audit, they found nothing out of order, but the episode scared me—not because we had anything to hide, but because I realized how vulnerable we were. All it took was the wrong assumption, a paperwork slipup, or an overzealous inspector, and everything I'd built could come crashing down. I had been flying blind, blissfully unaware of how easily things could spiral out of control if I wasn't paying attention to the details. It should have been a wake-up call.

Our bookkeeper filed a tax return that incorrectly showed that we owed the feds thirty grand, prompting an IRS lien. It took months to correct that mistake. I eventually realized that we had two silent partners—the state and federal governments—and they would get their pieces of the pie one way or another. Another wake-up call.

The owner of the Modesto lumberyard where we bought redwood for decks was always friendly, asking about our business and cheering us on. We were great customers. He wasn't so nice when I picked up the phone one harried morning. In a voice I hardly recognized, he said, "You owe us $10,000. Your account is past due. When you bring it up to date, we'll resume deliveries."

I sat, stunned, the receiver in my hand, and tried to breathe normally. I went through the mail I had ignored, maybe because I knew what I'd find—bad news I wasn't ready to face. Unpaid bills for lumber, nails, tools, gas, taxes, and a dozen other things totaled more than $50,000. We didn't have that much, or anything close to it in the bank. I had been running on delusion. I had bought into my own success story. Now, the reality was knocking, and I was panicked.

My partner was indifferent, almost impertinent. "What do you expect me to do about it?" I steadied my voice and told him we had to do something or we were out of business. The only thing I could think of was to ask our parents for help. I could imagine few things worse than admitting that Dad was right all along.

I drove up to Murphys in a near daze. I went into the store Dad managed, asked him to close his office door, and looked him in the eye. "I screwed up, Dad, and need your help." It was easier to say than I had feared. He didn't give me the I-told-you-so look I expected. He responded as one businessman to another. "Let's get this straightened out," he said. Our fathers each took out a $25,000 home equity loan. Vintage Hot Tubs repaid them, with interest, in a year.

That simple act hit me harder than any lecture ever could. For the first time, I understood that Dad wasn't just playing it safe; he was playing the long game. And maybe it was time I did the same.

By 1980, the surging popularity of hot tubs had attracted major players like Jacuzzi, HotSpring Spas, and Sundance Spas, which transformed hot tubs into mainstream products. At the same time, wooden barrel hot tubs were losing their charm—the wood fibers broke down from excessive chlorine, leaving hairlike strands floating in the water, and the barrels were prone to leaks. Acrylic and fiberglass spas offered greater convenience, durability, and ease of upkeep, with insulation for better energy efficiency. The market also became more standardized, with big-box stores like Costco offering spa packages at prices far lower than we could build them. Despite my insistence that redwood tubs looked nicer and were more comfortable, customers stopped listening—it was hard to argue against style and personal taste. It became clear I was fighting a losing battle. Staying in the hot tub business meant competing on price in a low-margin retail market, but even if I could, it would only lead to a race to the bottom—a direction that didn't appeal to me. If I wanted to survive, I had to make a major course correction.

## Entrepreneurial Life Lessons

- Ambition and drive are essential for any aspiring entrepreneur, but rushing forward without a plan can quickly lead to trouble.

- Entering into business partnerships too quickly often leads to costly and lasting regret.

- The best partnerships succeed when each partner leverages their unique strengths effectively.

- Luck can easily masquerade as skill—stay grounded and don't be fooled by it.

- Prioritize long-term goals over short-term wins to build enduring success.

# 5

# Pools

## Balancing Your Business and Yourself

usiness success requires constant adaptation—reading trends,
pivoting fast, being agile. I was in the right place at the right time
as Modesto surged. Its population neared 107,000 in 1980, up 75
percent in a decade, fueled by demand for Central Valley agricultural
products. Families flocked in from San Francisco and Sacramento,
seeking bigger and cheaper homes. Housing developments popped
up like crabgrass patches. And those new homeowners wanted
swimming pools.

A contractor called. His customers also wanted hot tubs alongside
their pools. Could we supply them? I jumped at the offer. It promised
a steady source of new business without making more sales calls. Sales
doubled almost overnight. We installed tubs as fast as Barden's crew
could make them. However, working for a general contractor had a

downside. While individual customers paid up front, the contractor didn't give us a cent until a pool project was complete. We often waited ninety days for a check. Barden was patient, but our freelance carpenters, plumbers, and electricians demanded cash on the spot, and suppliers of lumber and other supplies wanted payment in thirty days. I had to open a bank credit line—something I had hoped to avoid after our earlier financial fiasco. *Here we go again*, I thought.

I had an idea: Why not build swimming pools? While installing hot tubs, we watched them being built, and it didn't seem that complicated. You dug a big hole, lined it with steel rebar and concrete, connected plumbing and electrical wiring. Subcontractors did the work. General contractors sold the jobs, collected the checks, and parceled the money. Best of all, the pool construction business was cash flow positive. It required little capital. Homeowners put down a deposit and paid each phase in advance. With the custom hot tub market slowly drying up, what did we have to lose?

My partner liked the idea. His father, a longtime builder, was more cautious. "Do you know what you'd be getting into?" he said. He sounded like my dad. Countless contractors lost their shirts due to unexpected delays, rising material costs, or mismanaging subcontractor payments. He also pointed out that California required general contractors to have four years of experience in a related trade, which we didn't, as well as pass a knowledge test and have bonding and insurance. But against his better judgment, he agreed to be our frontman, sponsor, and guide. He helped us get a license and advised us on bidding, hiring subcontractors, and managing projects.

Changing our name from Vintage Hot Tubs to The Vintage Company, we entered the swimming pool business without capital, customers, or reputation. We were what people in the construction industry termed "windshield contractors"—builders who drove around in cars and didn't get their hands dirty. I would sell; my partner would oversee the work. No doubt there would be hiccups, but really, how could we lose?

Many people have said they couldn't have achieved great things had they known how hard it would be. Count me among them. It takes a combination of naivety and boldness to take on unknown challenges. The next five years earned me a PhD in the school of hard knocks. I learned to deal with no-show subcontractors, soothe irate customers, and reassure humorless bankers, several times coming within a hairsbreadth of going broke. Long hours and stress thinned my hair, meals on the run expanded my waistline, and I learned more about running an organization than I ever thought possible. And I did it alongside a partner who would tax the patience of a Zen master.

At up to $40,000, an in-ground swimming pool was the most expensive item most people would ever buy other than a house or car. How would we find customers? We had no showroom. How would I sell them? Unlike hot tubs, I had no model unit to show. How could we convince homeowners to trust a couple of twenty-something newbies? These were things I wished I had focused on in advance.

My partner spread the word at his church that we could build pools for less than the big contractors. Weeks went by without a bite. Our personal and business bank balances hovered near zero. Money worries had me staring at the ceiling in the wee hours.

A pharmacist and fellow church member named Ron Toy called. He had just bought a house in a new subdivision on the edge of town. I met him at his new abode, a one-story place with a patchy front yard. After a little small talk, I launched into the spiel I had spent hours practicing. "We've never built a pool," I admitted, "but we've watched the process up close. We know the subcontractors in Modesto—the excavators, rebar guys, and concrete sprayers. We know who's good and who's not. If you take a chance on us, you'll save a lot of money. And we'll give the job more time and attention than a builder juggling multiple projects."

Sensing his doubts as we stood in the backyard, my legs wobbled. After a long silence, he said, "Okay." I measured his yard and suggested where the pool should go and how long, wide, and deep it should be. We discussed some cosmetic details, and I proposed a price based on a spec sheet in my briefcase. He signed a boilerplate contract I had gotten from an office supply store. He walked me out to the gate, put his hand on the latch, and turned to me. "Bob," he said, "don't fuck this up." He smiled as he said it, and I chuckled along, but my stomach was tight. This wasn't about one job; it was about proving to myself, my dad, my partner's dad—basically my world—that I could succeed on my own terms. I felt the pressure down to my toes.

As Ron's pool took shape, more calls started coming in. Before long, I was doing half a dozen sales appointments a week. Charm was the only tool in my sales kit. I told our story, walked prospects through every phase of pool construction, looked them in the eye, and said, "Trust us. We're going to work hard to make it right for you. I would appreciate your vote of confidence." That puppy-dog appeal worked often enough to get us started. But despite offering bargain prices, I struggled to close deals. I was far from polished; my nervous awkwardness made homeowners doubt I could handle a project that would cost them a year's salary. Still, in the first month, I landed three contracts. Our biggest advantage, besides price, was that we weren't busy. The pool business was booming, and most builders were booked.

First impressions set expectations, and we couldn't afford to come off as sloppy. I knew instinctively that we were building a brand, although that term wasn't thrown about as much as it is today. I took pains to look professional and encouraged my partner to look presentable, a subliminal message that we knew our business.

Although convinced I was a natural salesman, I knew I needed to learn professional skills. I embarked on a journey of self-education to master the art and craft of selling. My car became a mobile classroom, a traveling MBA program. I hadn't been much of a student in high school and nixed college because I couldn't stomach the ideological blathering of professors. But this was different. I soaked up every bit of knowledge I could find. An ad in the *Modesto Bee* said anyone could become a great salesperson by mastering proven techniques. Fifty dollars bought a set of mail-order tape cassettes called "How to Master the Art of Selling Anything" by a Southern California real estate guru named Tom Hopkins.

Driving around from sales calls to job sites in my red Dodge Colt, I listened to Hopkins's inspiring story. After struggling as a real estate agent, a training seminar by J. Douglas Edwards turned his life around. By age twenty-seven, Hopkins was a millionaire, heading a company that sold 1,700 houses in a single year.

Virtually all pool builders in Modesto focused on price. They assumed that was all customers cared about. I went down that road too. In the beginning, I had little else to offer. But Tom Hopkins convinced me that was a race to the bottom. He pushed me to aim higher, charge premium prices, and focus on maximizing profit over revenue. And he told me how to do it. The secret, he said, was understanding customers and the deeper motives behind major purchasing decisions. We like to think we're rational, but emotions like love, fear, pleasure, and pain guide our choices. He used artfully phrased questions to guide conversations, build rapport, and transform hesitant prospects into buyers.

One of Hopkins's techniques was asking leading, or what he called "tie-down," questions. He might ask, "You would find that feature useful, wouldn't you?" or "This layout seems logical, doesn't it?" They prompted "yes" responses to create momentum toward a sale. Other open-ended questions revealed pain points and needs. He'd ask, "What do you value most in a new home?" or "How might this solution enhance your situation?" Such questions shifted the tone from selling to problem-solving, making clients feel acknowledged and understood.

The book *Frogs into Princes* introduced me to neurolinguistic programming, a way of understanding how people think, communicate, and behave. The authors, John Grinder, a linguistics professor, and Richard Bandler, a psychologist, showed how mirroring customers' body language, speech patterns, and tone of voice creates a sense of connection and gains trust. I learned everything I could about prospects before meeting them and used terms that echoed their occupations. Talking to a doctor, I'd diagnose a yard situation or cure a drainage problem. To a forklift operator, I'd liken the property to a warehouse floor plan and explain how I'd move things around to make room for the pool.

I began paying attention to what cars my prospective customers drove. A new Mercedes in the driveway? The prospect valued status and luxury. A five-year-old Volkswagen signaled practicality, as did how they landscaped their front yard and decorated their living rooms.

My competitors didn't do any of this stuff. They walked in, opened a loose-leaf notebook full of photos and charts, and said, "Here's what we can do and how much it will cost." I taught myself how to guide a sale through a process, like steps on a ladder. Each step of approval brought me closer to closing. I honed my sales techniques during two or three daily appointments. Sitting at kitchen tables, I'd sketch pool designs by hand on graph paper—what I privately called the "dog and pony show." I experimented with different approaches, refining my presentations and choreographing sales techniques in my mind. They had to seem natural, not memorized. If I didn't close a sale during the first meeting, I tried to be the last person a prospect met with before deciding. I would ask what they liked about the other bids, listen to their thoughts, offer ideas, and slowly guide them down a garden path.

I'd close the deal by asking for a $100 deposit to lock in the price. That deposit was small but key—it made them feel like they'd already bought something. Once they crossed that line, finalizing the plan was a formality. To get a building permit, I needed a licensed structural engineer to bless the plans. I usually took them to Greg, a young pro with a one-man shop in a strip mall. He'd review the plans for a hundred bucks and slap on a "wet stamp," as they called it in the trade. Then I'd head over to the building inspector's office, wait in line, and pay another hundred or so. Once I had the permit, it was time to pass the job to my partner to line up the subs.

Homeowners typically got three bids. Some people always go for the lowest one. But most pool shoppers were successful, with good jobs and new homes. They wanted a fair price, but they weren't bottom-feeders. They cared about quality and getting the job done right. Winning bids by being the cheapest wasn't sustainable when customers expected more than a low number. I had to convince them our low price didn't mean cutting corners. It was because we had no overhead—no fancy office, no high insurance bills, no truck payments, no payroll. We were hands-on, choosing the right subs to keep the quality up.

I shifted my sales approach. Instead of talking about how cheaply we could build pools, I focused on how cool we could make them. I steered conversations toward how the pool would enhance their lives—barbecues by the water on warm evenings, childhood birthday parties. I got them talking about their families and lifestyles. I also emphasized design. While other builders talked square footage, I talked about shape, how the pool would look at night with light reflecting off the water.

Other builders showed up with measuring tapes and calculators in hand. I kept my briefcase discreetly closed. I wanted every meeting to feel like a friendly chat, so they saw me as a trusted partner, not a lowball pitchman. Huddling with homeowners over kitchen tables, we brainstormed ideas and sketched them on a yellow legal pad. I asked, "What is your dream pool design?" "Do you envision something free-flowing or geometric?" "What would you like to see out your patio window at night?" I listened, drew rough images, and painted word pictures.

Over time, my heart-to-hearts with homeowners made me realize that we were talking about more than concrete, water, and aesthetics. A pool had a deeper meaning for them. The realization changed how I viewed my role and how I approached the construction business, and it set the stage for what was to come.

I visited an older couple at a luxurious home they were building outside town. Standing in the unfinished kitchen, I commented on how few people their age built such grand houses. The woman explained that she and her husband had recently come into money and wanted to create something to share with their grandchildren. Excusing herself momentarily, she approached a carpenter and politely pointed out that a patio door seemed skewed. As we resumed our conversation, the carpenter picked up a sledgehammer and angrily walloped the door frame. Startled, the woman closed her eyes, took a breath, and slowly walked back over. "Excuse me," she said in a soft voice. "You are stealing our dream."

Her words affected me. I focused less on practicalities and more on a swimming pool's impact on my customers' lives. I steered conversations to visions of twilight barbecues and alluded to relaxing by sparkling water after stressful days. I encouraged customers to share their life stories, their hopes and dreams. I painted mental images of kids doing cannonballs, little ones wrapped in beach towels eating hot dogs on the patio. We discussed how a pool would become a focal point of social gatherings and family life. I got the contract nine times out of ten, even when my price was significantly higher than the competition's. Before long, I was selling pools far more luxurious, expensive, and profitable than my competitors.

Of course, I had to get my foot in the door first. I elected to do little advertising. I had learned from selling hot tubs that word of mouth was the best form of marketing. Money was better spent on things that would get us talked about. When one person built a swimming pool, their neighbors wouldn't be far behind. Referrals would drive business. At poolside barbecues, someone would ask, "Who built this? Did they do a good job? What were they like to work with?" I wanted the answers to send customers my way. When my phone rang and someone said, "Mary and Joe love the pool you built for them," I knew I wouldn't have to do much selling; I would be taking an order.

Racking my brain for ideas on how to inspire word-of-mouth referrals, I read an article about Jan Carlzon, the CEO of Scandinavian Airlines (SAS), who was quickly transforming the once-ailing carrier into a model of customer service. He focused not only on the big stuff but also on small details that added up to a passenger's overall impression. He called them "memory moments." Identifying thirty points of customer contact—from booking to arrival—he concentrated on making each one a positive memory. His obsession with small details transformed the company and earned it Air Transport World's Airline of the Year award.

I wondered: How could I mimic that approach? I spent days analyzing every customer interaction throughout a pool project, from the initial inquiry to when a homeowner first entered the water. I identified two hundred touchpoints, from my knock at the front door to the arrival of a backhoe to sweeping the patio on the last day of construction. Each one could become a positive or negative memory.

How could I maximize the former and eliminate the latter? I sent small life jackets to children in families who had ordered a pool. I insisted subcontractors put a tarp on the driveway to avoid oil spots. I told crews to hose down patios at the end of each workday. I sent customers handwritten notes describing what we would do next.

One of the first things customers did on coming home was walk in their backyard to check things out. They would gaze at the property and visualize how the finished pool would look. I wanted them to be excited, to see the shape of their pool and the progress we were making. If they saw a mess, they would focus on that. I required my subcontractors to rake the yard and stack supplies and equipment neatly. Chances are, the contractor down the street wasn't doing that, and after a while, everyone on the block would notice.

Word of mouth cut both ways, of course. One bad experience could wipe out the goodwill earned from a dozen successful jobs. Building pools in half-acre backyards disrupted lives, especially for families with kids. Machines roared, workers wandered, and mud spread everywhere. Homeowners felt trapped in a seemingly endless process. Managing expectations became critical. I couldn't eliminate the hassle, but I could prepare customers by explaining the process and giving them a clear timetable.

Pool building is a linear process—a series of steps in a specific order. Workers mark the pool's shape. Excavators dig the hole, and dump trucks haul the dirt away. Steelworkers line the hole with rebar to create a sturdy framework. Plumbers and electricians install circulating pipes and wiring. Concrete workers spray and trowel gunite slurry to form the walls and floor. Masons apply plaster or tile on the hardened gunite. Plumbers and electricians come back to connect pumps, filters, and lights. Masons return to install sidewalks or decking. The process can take six to twelve weeks for a typical in-ground pool, assuming no major delays due to weather, supply chain issues, or subcontractor scheduling.

In our third year, we built 180 pools. Managing the work became a bigger challenge than selling the projects. The best subcontractors were in demand, so we had to court them to make them want to work with us rather than our competitors. They didn't want to trip over rocks and dirt from the previous sub. I hired cleanup crews to fill ditches and level the area around the pool, so everything was ready for the next phase.

As we piled on projects, it got harder to line up good subs, forcing us to use ones who weren't as skilled or reliable. That caused many problems. Managing them was like herding cats—they didn't always show up on time. Since one phase depended on the last, delays stalled progress and irritated homeowners, putting our reputation— and referrals—at risk. I found myself apologizing more, making excuses for no-shows. "Sorry, we thought we'd be there today, but another job ran long," I'd say. I hated those calls. When someone spent $40,000—a big sum back then—and asked, "You don't know when you're showing up?"—that was a call I didn't want to make.

My partner was supposed to keep everything on track but often failed. I promised a young mother we'd break ground on Tuesday morning. She called at ten, a hint of impatience in her voice: "Where is he?" Her kids, glued to the patio door, were eager to see the big machine.

I called my partner. "What's up with the digger?" I asked. "No problem," he said casually. "He'll get there eventually." Frustrated, I tried to call the tenant operator but got no answer. I finally tracked him down that night and learned the bitter truth: A competitor had paid him $500 extra to jump the line. "I didn't want to wake you," he lied. I called my partner again. "You're supposed to stay on top of this," I reminded him. I could almost see him shrug through the phone. "These things happen," he said. I hung up and yelled at the wall.

Surprises lurked on every project. A dump truck cracked a driveway, a tractor scraped siding, workers stomped through flower beds. Someone had to smooth things over. That someone was my partner—or at least it should have been. He knew construction and could oversee subcontractors, but he struggled to fix problems and calm frustrated customers. I wasn't sure if it was because he didn't understand how fragile our reputation was, couldn't read people, or just avoided conflict—maybe all three. I'd get calls from angry homeowners about delays, unsafe sites, or trashed yards. When a subcontractor messed up, my partner would downplay it, saying, "I took care of it," or "The homeowner's not upset." Meanwhile, the customer was ripping into me because I was the one who sold the job. The buck stopped with me.

I had to learn how to handle these situations. My approach was simple: When a customer got upset, I let them vent. It was hard not to jump in and defend myself, but I had to let them get it off their chest. Then I'd ask, "Is there anything else?" Usually, there wasn't. Finally, I'd ask, "What do you think we should do about it?" Unless the solution was unreasonable—like a refund—I'd agree. "Okay, that's what we'll do." It worked every time. But the stress still got to me.

Besides calling on prospects, I had to manage finances—collect money, pay subcontractors, and keep the books straight. I stayed on top of each project, making sure we had enough cash to keep everything moving. My partner had no interest in any of that. When I raised those issues, he'd smile, shrug, and shift the conversation to sports, food, or religion.

General contracting was a cash flow–intensive business. I used the customer's 10 percent down payment to pay the excavator to dig the hole and haul away the dirt. Once that was done, another 30 percent gave us working capital for the steelwork, plumbing, and spraying gunite to form the concrete walls. Another deposit funded the next phase. The flow of money never stopped—at least I hoped it wouldn't. With multiple projects going at once, managing it became a full-time job on top of my full-time sales job.

The endless juggling wore me out. I was stressed, sleepless, and always thinking about what could go wrong next. What problems was my partner ignoring, hiding, or downplaying? I lay awake at night, running numbers in my head, making sure we had enough to cover the next phase. The pressure never let up, but I kept pushing to keep it all afloat.

In the same way that I turned to Tom Hopkins for advice in salesmanship, I relied on Zig Ziglar to cope with the stress and challenges of running an enterprise that was growing almost faster than I could handle. His motivational book *See You at the Top* gave me a sense of control and honed and enhanced both my communication and selling skills, both critical for maintaining client relationships and staying motivated.

A former Mary Kay Cosmetics training whiz, Ziglar emphasized goal setting, positive thinking, and persistence. His first book manuscript was initially rejected by thirty-nine publishers, but once he found a publisher, the book went on to become a bestseller, helping establish him as one of the most influential motivational speakers and sales trainers of his era. Ziglar's philosophy centered around personal integrity, positive thinking, and helping others succeed as a path to success. He preached that success in business wasn't just about profits or sales but about developing character, faith, and gratitude—values that would shape my life, both professionally and personally.

I was particularly inspired by his emphasis on giving back. He said true success comes not just from achieving personal goals but from contributing to others' success, whether through mentorship, service, or kindness. In *Secrets of Closing the Sale*, Ziglar wrote, "You can have everything in life you want, if you will just help other people get what they want."

His teachings encouraged me to exercise generosity as a habit, comparing giving to building a muscle—something that strengthens over time through practice. He also emphasized that giving shouldn't be transactional: Never give to get; give because you have received. This perspective highlights how personal growth and fulfillment are deeply tied to how we serve and uplift others, whether in business or life. By aligning one's actions with these principles, Ziglar believed, one could not only cultivate better relationships but also create lasting success through positive ripple effects in one's communities and professional networks.

I thought of how my grandfather Campana helped people through his involvement in Freemasonry, the Shriners, and the Elks Club. Both my father and mother devoted many years to community service in their work with the hospital in Calaveras County. I have made a special effort to follow in their footsteps by mentoring individuals in their business lives—something I detail in subsequent chapters of this book.

In *The Psychology of Winning*, Denis Waitley preached the importance of discipline, self-confidence, and achieving a winner's mindset. His practical advice on developing habits that foster success helped me stay mentally sharp and resilient, manage pressure, avoid burnout, and adopt a long-term vision. A former Navy officer and consultant, he assured me that every entrepreneur hits potholes on the highway to success and provided "self-talk" exercises to replace negative thoughts with positive ones.

Together, Ziglar and Waitley provided not just technical insights into sales and business growth but also emotional tools for self-mastery. These are crucial for balancing the demands of a fast-growing enterprise without falling apart under the weight of responsibility. Their teachings aligned perfectly with the mindset I needed: to lead effectively, adapt quickly, and grow personally and professionally.

In 1983, Tony Robbins had not yet achieved global recognition as a motivational speaker. That came later, with his infomercials and the release of his "Personal Power" tapes in the 1990s. But he was building his career through Southern California seminars teaching entrepreneurs neurolinguistic programming techniques.

I liked Robbins's up-from-nothing story: dropping out of high school at seventeen to support a troubled family, a chance encounter with Jim Rohn, a well-known personal development coach, and a mentor–mentee relationship with Rohn that changed his life. He preached that most obstacles in life are psychological and that you can train your mind to overcome them. He promised to help people find their internal "driving forces." His so-called fire walking seminars urged attendees to walk barefoot over hot coals as a metaphor for overcoming fear and achieving breakthroughs. Although that sounded a little scary, they were so popular that I wanted to attend one if I could find the time in my hectic schedule.

My chance came that fall, when the seasonal pool business slowed down. Robbins scheduled a seminar at the San Jose Convention Center, an hour away. I sent in my check for $500. Hundreds packed the coliseum. Robbins, an imposing figure at six foot seven, riled them up with stories about his life. He segued into insights on neurolinguistic programming, goal setting, and unlocking potential. At midmorning, I watched him pour flammable fluid on a long stack of oak logs and toss a match. At the end of the day, he led us all back to what was now a long stretch of red cinders and asked us to remove our shoes and socks. We were going to walk on fire. "Don't worry," he said. "We have ambulances standing by just in case. Ha-ha."

People talked nervously and put on brave fronts. A few shuffled into tents for little pep talks. As I approached the glowing embers, Tony said, "Close your eyes and imagine you're walking on cool grass." I felt the heat but no pain. On the other side, somebody showed me a thermometer reading 800 degrees and sprayed my feet with a garden hose. If I could do that, I could do anything.

## Entrepreneurial Life Lessons

- Tackling new challenges demands a mix of bold action and blissful naivety.

- First impressions are powerful; they establish expectations that can last indefinitely.

- Continuously self-educate to refine and enhance your professional skills over time.

- Focus less on logistics and more on how you improve customers' lives.

- Clearly manage customers' expectations from the beginning to avoid future misunderstandings.

- When customers get upset, fairly or not, let them vent, then ask how you can make it right.

- You need to develop the right emotional mindset to balance the weight of responsibility of running a business.

# 6

# The Roaring '80s

## Managing Staff and Expectations

The 1980s were a decade of ambition and chaos. As my business grew, managing staff became a juggling act, clients tested my patience, and partnerships sometimes felt like a wrestling match. Each challenge forced me to sharpen my instincts and figure out who I really was—not just as an entrepreneur, but as a person trying to stay upright.

Doubling down, I threw myself into the business, convinced that working harder would keep me ahead of the curve. But as the company grew, cracks showed. I made costly mistakes and lay awake calculating cash flow. I had to learn how to manage an enterprise that was becoming much bigger than myself, but I didn't feel comfortable delegating anything.

A growing family provided motivation. On October 10, 1981, I married Lynna Denice Horman, a twenty-two-year-old brunette I had been dating since the early hot tub days. I met her at a restaurant where she was a hostess and persuaded her to greet customers part time at our little showroom behind the coffee shop. There was little traffic, but it was the only way to get her to hang around. Before long, I spent more time flirting than working. She reluctantly agreed to dinner, and things went from there.

Lynna had a level-headed and practical approach to life. She grew up as one of seven children in a family where money was always tight. After graduating from Modesto High in 1976, she became an instructional aide in the city's schools. My partner was my best man at the wedding in the old St. Stanislaus Catholic Church in downtown Modesto, where Lynna had grown up. Then we took off on a six-week honeymoon through Hawaii, Japan, Hong Kong, Malaysia, India, Germany, and Austria. I hoped my wanderlust was contagious.

We bought a small house on Semple Street in a working-class neighborhood downtown. The rapid-fire births of Annie, Katrina, and Audrey in 1984, 1986, and 1988 prompted a move three miles north to a larger ranch house on Wellington Drive, in a leafy professional neighborhood. We lived simply there, barbecuing by the backyard pool on summer evenings. After the upheavals and economic uncertainty of the 1960s and '70s, we wanted to give our children a warm, supportive, emotionally connected family environment. Lynna and I shared a desire to expose them to the world that we had discovered in our travels and give them a strong religious grounding and the educational opportunities that we hadn't had, or in any event hadn't pursued. The Vintage Company could make that happen.

The 1984 Reagan boom, combined with falling interest rates, turbocharged the swimming pool business. In peak spring and summer seasons, we often had two dozen pools under construction at any given time. Managing all the moving parts—collecting deposits, coordinating subcontractors, and ensuring payments went out on time—was a logistic challenge. I hated the drudgery of sending invoices, writing checks, and keeping track of money, so I hired a full-time bookkeeper. That gave me time to focus on the big picture and consider where I wanted the company to go. I had gotten that far without much strategic thought, instead moving on inertia, reacting to events, and responding to opportunities as they arose. Now, at age thirty, with the responsibility of a family, I wanted a clearer path, a long-term destination, and a plan to get there.

At Lynna's suggestion, I signed up for a night class in finance at Modesto Junior College. The dozen or so students were a mix of dreamers and small-business owners. The subject was alien and intimidating. Despite being the part owner of a company with a million dollars in annual revenue, I had only the most basic grasp of accounting: Money came in and went out. It was a short-term view, not much different from that of a family living paycheck to paycheck.

It's funny how things we don't pay much attention to, like electricity or water, gain new significance when you look hard at them, viewing them from a slightly different perspective. I hadn't paid particular attention to the stream of money flowing through my business. Sure, more was good, and the faster it came in the better. It just didn't occur to me that closely observing the flow rate and how it varied over time was a useful management activity. But the instructor, a young man named William Weller, explained that measuring and tracking cash flow provided valuable, even critical, information. It was an insight into the business's health, like taking its blood pressure. Variability in the flow rate wasn't random; there was usually a discernible pattern that could help an owner make better financial and strategic decisions. He quoted Peter Drucker's book *Innovation and Entrepreneurship: Practice and Principles*, which said that "entrepreneurs believe that profit is what matters most. But profit is secondary. Cash flow matters most."

Predictable cash flow unlocked one of a business's most powerful tools: credit. Strategically employed debt not only smoothed out daily and seasonal variables but also enabled growth that was impossible to attain by relying only on funds in a company's checking account. The realization transformed how I viewed business and, over the next few years, altered the trajectory of my company and my life.

Weller and I became friends. We talked often after class about the state of the national and local economy. I sought his advice on growing the company and the challenges of managing a bigger enterprise. There were only so many hours in the day, and I was about maxed out. He said fast-growing start-ups invariably outgrew the founder-run management styles. He suggested I read about how other companies made that transition and how they worked.

He recommended the bestselling tome *In Search of Excellence* by two McKinsey management consultants. Tom Peters and Robert H. Waterman identified "principles of excellence" that set companies apart from the competition. Although it was about giant multinationals like IBM, Hewlett-Packard, and Procter & Gamble, smaller companies could learn a lot. Success wasn't just about size, Weller said, "it was about focus, innovation, and culture, all those things." Forty years later, I can't pinpoint specific lessons I learned. Still, I came away inspired by how those successful companies thought beyond numbers and focused on people—customers, suppliers, and employees. I resolved to do a better job of that.

I was determined to rely less on subcontractors and hire full-time crews. Jobs would be easier to schedule and manage; we could build pools faster, with more control and fewer mix-ups. Customers would be happier. It would move us to the forefront of the pool construction business. I imagined fleets of trucks emblazoned with

The Vintage Company logo. We would be visible, at the forefront of the business.

But it would also be a gamble, because it's hard to reverse course once you're on that path. We were busy, but while pools could be built year-round, there was seasonal variability. Demand softened in the fall and picked up in early spring. It would be expensive: salaries, machinery, and equipment alone would require a lot of cash. Could we sustain a steady enough cash flow?

My partner was on board. He thought assembling teams of skilled workers would be easy, that many subcontractors would prefer a full-time job over constantly wondering where their next meal was coming from. "No problem," he said. But that was his response to almost every question, and I wasn't sure how much he had thought things through.

By 1988, I was determined and confident enough to dip my toe in the water. Where to start? Digging holes was the first step in pool construction, but it required heavy machinery. We'd need an excavator to handle the main work—actually two, because they broke down frequently. We'd want a plate compactor to stabilize the pool base after excavation. And at least two dump trucks so that while one was dumping dirt, another could be filled. Otherwise, the high-salary operator would sit there waiting, munching on a bag of Doritos. That was a hundred thousand dollars right there. Our monthly cash flow would easily qualify us for sufficient bank credit, but I wasn't ready to take on that debt until I was sure this in-house scheme was going to work.

Plumbing, steel, and electrical work—jobs that didn't require much machinery—was a wiser place to begin. Typically, these tasks were handled by three different subcontractors, but I didn't want to pay for three separate crews. That's when I had a brainstorm inspired by the book I was reading at the time called *The Goal* by

Eliyahu M. Goldratt, an Israeli physicist, management consultant, and author. His Theory of Constraints was a methodology for improving organizational performance. He argued, among other things, that overspecialization and segmentation were inefficient; giving workers broader responsibilities could get more done faster and cheaper. This idea went against the prevailing management wisdom that prioritized specialization, but I figured it was worth a shot. (Goldratt also influenced my thinking in other ways, which I will get more into shortly.)

I assembled a small crew—a steelworker, a plumber, an electrician, and five laborers—and told them to go in as soon as a subcontractor dug the hole. They had no instructions other than to figure out how to work together and get the job done. It was a gamble; eight tradesmen scrambling around on a pit the size of a tennis court, trying to keep out of each other's way, could have turned into a *Keystone Cops*–style disaster. My partner would be there to supervise, but that gave me little comfort.

It was a tricky stage of the pool construction because a building inspector had to sign off on everything and usually found something to nitpick: An electric wire would be too close to the dirt; rebar spacing would be a little too wide. Subcontractors would drag their feet about coming back to fix things, which slowed things down and annoyed customers. I hoped the new team system would work better. I said, "If there's a problem, I don't care whose fault it is—just fix it." The first project went off without a hitch, and the team members gave themselves high fives.

I expanded our capabilities step-by-step. Our next team installed the coping stones that capped the wall with a smooth edge. Another team poured and leveled the concrete walkways and patios. They needed a heavy-duty truck with a cement mixer on the back, but that was cheap compared to outsourcing the job. I weighed each investment carefully. The most expensive subcontractors, like excavation and gunite spraying, were the last ones we replaced because of the high equipment cost.

The integrated team approach was one of my smartest management decisions. Blending the expertise of specialists working alongside lower-skilled laborers maximized productivity. It made the pool-building process faster and more economical. It encouraged me to vertically integrate more functions. I hired masons and bought a truck to carry their tools and supplies. I used a bank credit line to acquire a couple of used excavators, trailers to carry them, and a small dump truck to clean up construction debris. I bought a small parcel of land to store dirt for reuse on future projects. As I felt more confident, I bought front-end loaders and more dump trucks and built a garage to service them.

The Vintage Company grew to almost one hundred employees over the next five years. On the outside, things looked rosy. People praised my business genius; I smiled and accepted kudos, knowing better than to believe my own PR. But in many ways, the journey was more tumultuous than anything before. Learning to manage a team of that size, with crew leaders, site supervisors, four accountants, and three pool salesmen, was a steep curve. In theory, my partner would have taken on a lot of that burden, but he showed little interest in anything that wasn't on the job site, and even then I had to communicate directly with his subordinates.

One thing every boss learns quickly is that getting accurate information is hard. Employees often tried to shield me from mistakes. They didn't want me busting their chops for screwing up. That left me handling angry calls from customers. I'd be defensive, trying to explain things I knew nothing about. And the customers were usually right. I should have known. I took their money with the promise of getting the job done right. I was responsible for whatever happened.

Construction had many moving parts—schedules, materials, delays. It always felt like we were putting out fires. I wanted to figure out where the real bottlenecks were—the hidden roadblocks that slowed us down. I didn't want to just treat the symptoms; I wanted a smoother flow, where everything worked better together. I needed to see the big picture while still focusing on the details.

The more I thought about it, the more I realized that a pool-building operation was essentially a mobile factory. Instead of doing everything under one roof, we brought the factory to our customers' backyards. We'd dig the hole, put in the plumbing, set up the steel, run the electrical, then move to the next home and do it all over again. Why couldn't the same techniques manufacturers used to streamline operations, eliminate errors, and address problems work for us?

My search for insights, answers, and solutions led me down a rabbit hole of manufacturing theory. Once again, I turned to Eliyahu M. Goldratt's *The Goal*. Unlike most management texts, he used a fictional narrative to explain his Theory of Constraints, which was primarily a way of identifying and addressing bottlenecks that stalled or sidetracked a project. Goldratt offered no advice specific to pool construction, but if I could boil his theory down into one bit of practical advice, it was this: Don't try to improve efficiency with broad exhortations from the top. Focus on identifying the most serious bottlenecks and addressing them one at a time. Let the others be, or you'll go nuts.

Goldratt's advice neatly dovetailed with three other management books I was reading. W. Edwards Deming's *Out of the Crisis* (1982) outlined how statistical quality control and the Japanese philosophy of *kaizen*—continuous improvement—revitalized Japanese industry after World War II. Another book, *Total Quality Control* (1951) by Armand V. Feigenbaum, preached that quality was everyone's job, from top management to the factory floor. A third, *The Machine That Changed the World* (1990), by three experts from the Massachusetts Institute of Technology, detailed how Toyota's "lean manufacturing" system transformed production processes worldwide. All three books emphasize that achieving quality and efficiency requires a comprehensive, organization-wide commitment to continuous improvement and collaborative processes. Could I do that within my little construction company, or was I delusional? I decided to give it a shot.

Toyota's "Five Whys" problem-solving technique particularly fascinated me. It focused on digging deep to find the root cause of issues rather than applying quick fixes. This method encourages a thorough investigation to prevent problems from recurring. For example, if a car's paint job came out flawed, the team would ask why. The first answer might be that the paint isn't sticking; a second "why" might reveal that the mixture wasn't prepared correctly. A further why might show that the mixing machine wasn't calibrated properly, and asking why again might uncover that maintenance was delayed. By repeatedly asking why, the team could address the root issue rather than just the symptoms.

Inspired, I tried to implement lean manufacturing techniques in my company. Eliminating waste, optimizing processes, and embracing continuous improvement made so much sense to me, and I was sure they would transform our productivity. But when I used the "Five Whys" with my team, they looked at me with barely concealed exasperation, like parents dealing with a curious five-year-old. I could almost see them checking their watches.

In hindsight, I realized I'd missed an important point: my audience. My foremen and crew chiefs had worked their way up from jobs as dishwashers, janitors, and field workers. To them, work was straightforward—do the job, get paid, and go home. They weren't interested in dissecting tasks or analyzing efficiency. For them, work was a means to an end, not something to perfect.

To complicate things further, many were Spanish-speaking immigrants new to the country, and the language gap went beyond vocabulary. They'd nod, smile, and say, "Yes, yes, I understand," but the next day, I'd find that nothing had really changed—or sometimes had gotten worse.

Looking back, I see that it was hopeless from the start. I thought sharing what I knew would inspire everyone, but nods and smiles don't always mean understanding. Introducing new concepts to people unfamiliar with your way of thinking can lead to polite responses—out of respect or even job security concerns—but it doesn't necessarily mean they grasp it. The lesson here? Think of your workforce as your audience. It's not what you say but what gets communicated.

In any case, I had bigger things to worry about. Within months of fully committing to integration, a recession clobbered real estate and, by extension, the pool business. Amid the collapse of more than one thousand US savings and loan institutions, rising interest rates, the first Gulf War, and rising oil prices, homeowners were in no mood to buy luxuries, and banks were in no mood to lend.

Meanwhile, I was trying to secure capital to buy excavators, dump trucks, concrete mixers, tile saws, scaffolding, and storage containers. Every two steps step forward was followed by one and a half back. Frequent equipment breakdowns squeezed margins.

Despite high cash flow, solvency was touch and go. Late one Friday in 1990, I realized that the weekly payroll exceeded my bank balance by $8,000. My stomach churned, knowing checks would bounce unless I covered them by Monday. The only hope was to sell at least three pools over the weekend and quickly deposit the 10 percent deposits. Was that even possible? I desperately scheduled back-to-back appointments with anyone who had expressed the slightest interest in building a pool. Ringing doorbells, I steeled myself to seem calm, composed, and confident. People, like dogs, sense stress. Sunday night, as a client walked me to the door, a third deposit in my pocket, I glimpsed myself in a hall mirror. I thought of Friedrich Nietzsche's words in his book *Twilight of the Idols*: "That which does not kill us makes us stronger." If he only knew.

The push to maintain quality on tight deadlines strained relationships with clients, suppliers, managers, and employees. Moments of doubt and frustration tested my resolve and patience. The prospect of failure terrified me. No one in such a situation views it as a learning opportunity or a badge of honor. In my case it would mean not just public embarrassment but also the loss of my business, and in some way my independence. The thought of asking my dad for help again was horrifying. Letting down Lynna and my young daughters was worse. For some people, fear is paralyzing—but it kept me going. I survived because I was too scared to fail.

Somehow, we clawed through. By 1993, The Vintage Company had twenty trucks and almost one hundred employees. We were one of three contractors in the Modesto area that could construct swimming pools without using subs. Having full control over a project was a significant competitive advantage. I could confidently promise to start construction on a specific date and complete it within a specified period. I focused my sales pitch on the benefit of relying on a vertically integrated builder rather than on a loose affiliation of freelancers.

I rented a house that we turned into our showroom. We parked our trucks in a big yard next door. Standing in front of a fleet of trucks and skilled crews, I could demonstrate the scale and reliability of our operations. This added a layer of credibility and reassured customers that I had the resources to deliver on our promises.

It catapulted us to another level. Homeowners were willing to pay a premium for that security.

The key to any business is the people you bring in. We hired skilled technicians and supervisors to manage projects. Our reputation for fair treatment and competitive pay attracted workers. Recruiting became less of a challenge. Many experienced workers in the Central Valley construction industry felt undervalued or overlooked for promotions and knocked on my door. They often brought in underlings they knew and were confident would make their jobs easier. Agricultural laborers, many of them undocumented with fake Social Security numbers, saw construction as a step up. They often learned skills on the job and moved up to crew chiefs.

We started by poaching employees from other builders. If we needed a project manager, we knew there was always someone out there with a burr under his saddle. He'd been with his company for fifteen years and never got that promised trip to Hawaii, or whatever. When we heard from subcontractors that someone wasn't happy where they were, we'd reach out, offer a raise, and basically bribe him to join us. That new project manager would know crew leaders looking for better opportunities, guys he liked working with to make his job easier, and he'd bring them over. It went like that—scraping guys from other companies. I'd say, "Call Joey, see if you can get him to work for us." Over time, we sorted the wheat from the chaff and ended up with the best guys. Our crews hit the supply houses every morning, grabbing grout, mortar, pipes—the basics. That's where they'd bump into guys from other companies, talk, and compare notes. Word spread fast that we paid more, treated people well, and had good equipment. Once that cycle kicked in, skilled workers knocked at our door.

We hired a lot of undocumented workers. Hispanic culture valued hard work and respect. These guys were hungry for jobs and eager to learn because they knew skills meant better pay. In California, especially in construction, you couldn't get much built without Hispanic labor. They came here chasing a better life and worked hard for it. We started them on cleanup crews—raking, washing, handling basic tasks that were hard to mess up. Jaime, one of our trusted foremen, would assess them, spend a few months figuring out their strengths. Some guys ended up on tile work, others digging pools. Jaime was the gatekeeper, making sure we put them where they'd excel.

Ninety-nine percent of hiring is about attitude, not skills. You can train someone in the skills, but you can't teach them attitude. Either they want to do a good job or they don't. It took me time to learn that. I wanted to believe the best in everyone, but negativity drags you down. You've got to let things play out and see who's cut out for the work.

Everyone had a strength; we moved guys through different crews to find them. One guy might be great at setting tile, another at tying steel, and another could be a solid plumber. Eventually, we found a guy who could schedule projects like a chessboard. He knew the phases of a pool build and kept everything on track.

One unexpected challenge involved workers' compensation premiums, which climbed so high that they put us at a competitive disadvantage. I pulled my hair out trying to figure out why and then discovered that some workers learned how to game the system; they intentionally sprained a wrist or faked a back injury to collect a big workers' comp payout. It took a while, but I finally found the solution in an incentive game called Safety Bingo. At every job site, I put a twenty-dollar bill in a glass jar and added another daily. After a while, it contained several hundred dollars. Each employee got a numbered bingo card and marked off a square daily. The first one to hit bingo won the jackpot. If an accident happened, I took all the money out and started over. Everyone liked the game. When they gathered, eyeing the money jar at day's end, there was a lot of joking and ribbing, a sense of team camaraderie. But there was also unspoken peer pressure to follow safety rules; no one wanted to be the one to break the accident-free streak. The strategy worked; premiums edged back down. But I was sure of one thing: Another unpleasant surprise lurked, sight unseen. Running a small business was like Whac-A-Mole.

Money and emotions are a volatile mix. If I got three or four pieces of information in a given morning that cost me thousands of dollars because someone didn't do what he was supposed to, everyone felt the heat. When things didn't go my way, I acted on emotion. I'd get angry and yell. I'd take it out on someone, even though it might not have been his fault. Over time, I realized that was hurting morale and productivity.

What was the target of my outrage going to think about all day? It wasn't how he loved being part of a great organization. He was going to seethe with resentment, obsess over how unfair I was, wonder if he should look for another job. I was pushing him away. After an outburst, I'd feel regret for hours, asking myself, "Why did I do that?" I knew things had to change if I was going to be an effective boss. That meant learning to take a deep breath and say, "How am I going to get this problem solved? How am I going to turn this situation around?"

For that insight, I credit a guy named Joe, whose last name I have long forgotten. He came in from Las Vegas to manage the construction of a three-hundred-room, thirteen-story hotel in Modesto. We got the contract to build an elevated swimming pool. It was a complicated commercial contract. I worried that I had bitten off more than I could chew. When Joe called me into his office on day one, I was terrified, expecting a veiled threat about what would happen if I screwed up.

A huge construction flowchart covered the wall behind his desk. Joe got up, shook my hand, and sat beside me. In a calm voice, he said, "Bob, I need your help. We want to make sure that this pool and the hotel open on time. We selected you out of all the other pool builders, and I want you to know how much confidence I have in you. As you can see, I have a lot on my plate. I hope you can solve problems on your own. But we're on the same team, and I want you to know that I'm here if you need me."

I was awed that this important man took the time to sit down with me, have this bonding conversation, and then humble himself to tell me that he needed my help to get this job done. It was a big lesson to me—putting the people who are doing the work on a little bit of a pedestal and showing them that you trust them to do their jobs.

I didn't regard myself as a control freak, though I had heard that phrase whispered. But my background as a hands-on entrepreneur who built the business from the ground up made it hard to step back. The early days of running everything myself had forced me to rely on my own instincts and attention to detail, knowing that every decision directly impacted the company's survival and reputation. Coming from a family with a strong work ethic no doubt reinforced the idea that I needed to make sure everything was done just right. And feeling like I had to keep an eagle eye on my partner kept me on high alert. I felt like the company was running me rather than the other way around.

I'd hover over a site manager, double-checking every detail of a pool layout or inspecting materials that a foreman had already approved. I even gave input on scheduling, telling crew chiefs when to pour concrete or where to park trucks. These were tasks I'd hired capable people to handle, yet I couldn't resist getting involved. It was a habit that undermined the very trust and independence I wanted my team to develop.

It took years to fully change my ways, but I finally did so in the late 1990s, with the help of Robert Kiyosaki, whose book *Rich Dad, Poor Dad* stressed the importance of mastering delegation. Kiyosaki emphasized building systems, leveraging other people's time and skills, and focusing on high-value activities rather than getting bogged down in day-to-day tasks. He contrasted the mentality of the "poor dad," who traded time for money, with the "rich dad," who understood how to make money work for him. This shift in mindset helped me realize that the key to growing my business wasn't just about working harder—it was about working smarter. I looked at successful construction men in my community. Most of them weren't doing everything themselves. They had crews, office staff, and specialists handling different parts of the business. At a certain point, I realized my time was more valuable spent growing the company than getting stuck in the weeds.

I eventually got to the point that instead of barking orders to crew leaders, I'd say, "Hey, guys, I need your help on this project." I encouraged them to take responsibility, gave them the authority to solve problems independently without calling me, made them feel like managers, made them proud to be leaders, and wanted them to show me they were worthy of my confidence. I am certain that few things I did as an owner had a more positive impact on my business.

Being a hands-off manager might have been good for business, but I had become the kind of desk-bound administrator I once mocked, shuffling paper, paying bills, and fretting over cash flow. I was at the center of a never-ending storm that sometimes felt like a Category 5 hurricane. My phone rang constantly; every call brought a new problem. A field supervisor on one line told me his excavator was on life support while a homeowner on the other line gave me an earful about cracked concrete. There was no way on God's green earth I could do everything. Endless distractions made it hard to think about next week, let alone next year. Stress affected my demeanor. I was always angry. I tried not to take it home, but it hurt when I sensed that one of my daughters hesitated to ask a simple question for fear it would set me off.

Stephen Covey, like Kiyosaki, came to my rescue. His book *The 7 Habits of Highly Effective People* also helped me understand the art—or was it the science?—of delegation. He distinguished between "gofer delegation," where bosses told people what to do step-by-step, and "stewardship delegation," which focused on results rather than methods. He said the first was management poison; the second built strong and resourceful teams. It empowered individuals to take responsibility for their tasks and encouraged them to develop methods to achieve the desired results. This approach not only enhanced productivity, he said, but also fostered a culture of trust, growth, and teamwork.

One of Covey's most useful lessons was that all matters were not equally urgent or important and that it was necessary to learn the difference. Treating them alike led to bad decisions and endless anxiety.

He suggested sorting tasks and activities into four categories:

Urgent and important (medical crises)
Important but not urgent (strategic planning)
Urgent but not important (most phone calls)
Not urgent and not important (reading *Dilbert* in the comics)

Covey said successful people prioritized number-two-important-but-not-urgent matters like planning, preparation, and personal development. When they did that, they (unsurprisingly) encountered fewer urgencies.

The system sounded like just the ticket, but I found it unwieldy in practice and nearly gave up. Who had time to label each little task? Eventually, I decided I was interpreting Covey's system too literally. He wasn't suggesting meticulously categorizing everything I did; he simply wanted me to shift my mindset, recognize patterns in my life, and spend more time in the "important but not urgent" quadrant and less in the "urgent and important" zone. Less time firefighting meant more for planning and personal growth. He just wanted me to think carefully as I managed money. Once I figured that out, it became second nature. I encouraged everybody in the office and the field to use the system. I wasn't sure whether they did, but they no doubt liked having a calmer boss.

Having full-time crews, for all the headaches, opened an income stream I hadn't foreseen: landscape construction. Most pool builders didn't do it because it required additional expertise and resources. Pulling everything together was a complex process—far more involved than pool building. Pool contractors usually started out working for other builders, doing tasks like digging holes or installing plumbing. By the time they earned their licenses, they had experience in pool construction but not in landscaping. They could do rebar, concrete, and plumbing, but taking on an entire backyard transformation was a bridge too far.

Our vertically integrated operation could deliver everything needed for a dream backyard, like something from *Sunset* magazine.

We had the resources and skills to offer a one-stop solution, guiding clients from permits to finishing touches—the ability to deliver a pool and landscape in one shot. Our carpentry crew built arbors, gazebos, wood structures, and decks. Our masonry team crafted fireplaces, barbecue systems, pizza ovens, and stonework, including patios, retaining walls, and benches. Our landscapers handled irrigation, planting, and final touches. Landscape construction became not only a way to sell pools but a profit center in itself.

Since the early days, I had created visions of lavish yards to sell pools: Japanese maples swaying in the breeze, rolling hills, wooden gazebos for quiet reading and romance. Never mind that it was hard to achieve all that on a half-acre suburban plot. But in the twenty years since we had begun selling hot tubs, the greater Modesto area had gotten richer. Successful farming families, business owners, and executives, along with legacy wealth like that of the extended Gallo wine family, flaunted their prosperity by building larger homes and expanding estates in neighborhoods like Del Rio and Riverbank. They were willing to invest in luxury outdoor living spaces, and my small army of skilled and unskilled workers allowed me to bring those fantasy worlds to life. We were invited to bid on jobs we wouldn't have been considered for five years earlier. A nice pool might cost $45,000, and high-end landscaping projects typically ran from $100,000 to $250,000.

I learned everything I could about landscaping, working closely with independent professionals until I gained the expertise and industry network to design everything on my own. I learned how to "paint" with light, using uplighting and downlighting on trees, bushes, and architectural elements to create an atmosphere with shadows and highlights.

My landscape work revealed an artistic side I hadn't previously recognized. I had sketched countless pool designs at kitchen tables, but as the projects grew bigger, so did my vision. Frederick Law Olmsted I was not, but I loved reimagining flat Central Valley backyards as miniature Central Parks—rolling landscapes with views that hinted at the distant Sierra peaks. Over time, I grew confident enough to handle all the design work myself, no outside help needed.

Few pool contractors in the Modesto area could manage comprehensive projects like ours. They cobbled together alliances—partnering with landscaping firms and using subcontractors for gazebos and pergolas. This approach often created coordination challenges, inconsistencies in quality, and longer timelines, as each aspect of the project had to be scheduled and managed separately. Our integrated model ensured a seamless experience for clients, making it hard for competitors to make direct price comparisons. By the late 1990s, we were landing a dozen quarter-million-dollar jobs and four or five half-million-dollar jobs annually—big money at the time in California's Central Valley.

Managing my sprawling construction mini empire increased my management workload. As in the past, I turned to virtual mentors, aka visionary authors, for advice. I tested the patience and good humor of Lynna and my four daughters—Caroline had come along in 1994—by immersing myself in books after dinner. *The E-Myth* by Michael Gerber was at the top of the pile. The book title stood for "entrepreneurial myth—the notion that small business owners are natural entrepreneurs." Gerber, a business consultant, drew from years of experience working with company founders who, like me, were overwhelmed by day-to-day operations. He said most of them crashed and burned because they focused solely on technical tasks. A restaurant owner spent too much time in the kitchen, the auto repair entrepreneur too much time under hoods. In doing so, they neglected essential things like finances and planning. In his book, Gerber said, "they worked *in* the business instead of *on* the business."

That message struck home for me for a couple of reasons. First, it made me realize that my obsession with selling was distracting me from my real job: running a company. I couldn't do both.

Second, *The E-Myth* helped me understand my partner a little better. He wasn't lazy; he just saw himself as a construction guy, happiest working in a hole in the ground alongside plumbers, electricians, and rebar crews. Knowing this didn't change anything, but it made me a little more understanding—though not accepting—of his disinterest in business affairs.

Gerber also enlightened me on another aspect of growing a business that greatly influenced me in the years ahead. He said a successful company wasn't just about doing something well; it was about doing it repeatedly with the same result each time. Growth was about scalability, and scale required a system. Companies needed standardized processes to ensure consistent quality and efficiency without the owner's constant oversight. It was essentially the McDonald's-style franchise model. Its hamburgers were hardly culinary art, but customers knew what to expect. Ray Kroc made it a world leader by being predictable. He broke operations into simple tasks that anyone could do: Put a patty on the grill and push a red button. When the buzzer goes off, flip it. He optimized and documented every task that could be done with minimal training.

Construction wasn't fast food, but I took Gerber's point and decided to give it a shot. Most of my employees had little education and limited skills, performing the same tasks repeatedly, so the approach made sense in a practical way. I explained Gerber's ideas to my partner, encouraging him to outline each step of the construction phases. I advised gathered site managers and crew chiefs to do the same. Few had high school educations, and most spoke only broken English, but they nodded politely as I described the benefits of structured processes. Whether they fully understood or intended to follow through, I couldn't be sure; I wasn't down in the ditches with them, so I had no real way of knowing.

Over time, I noticed our teams working more efficiently and coordinating more fluidly. In retrospect, I doubt it had much to do with my attempt at micromanagement. More likely, the gains came from experience and familiarity with the work. Repetition naturally brought a rhythm to the job that no checklist or process guide could create. The improvements had less to do with structured steps and more with each team member getting comfortable with the work and finding their own flow.

While assembly-line predictability was appealing, it wasn't necessarily achievable—at least not in the way Ray Kroc envisioned it. Everyone along the management chain has to fully understand the concept and buy into it, which is rarely the case on a California construction site. However, Gerber gave me a new framework for thinking about my business and how I might expand it. That set the stage for the next phase in the company's growth.

## Entrepreneurial Life Lessons

- Profit may be the ultimate goal, but steady cash flow sustains growth.

- Blended teams of specialists and generalists achieve more than isolated experts.

- Unseen bottlenecks are often the greatest barriers to productivity and progress.

- When hiring, prioritize a positive attitude over technical experience—it makes all the difference.

- Successful entrepreneurs focus on building their businesses, not getting lost in daily tasks.

- Scalable systems drive sustainable growth far better than aiming for technical perfection.

- Delegation is essential; micromanagement erodes trust and undermines team independence and strength.

# 7

# Exit

## Seeking the Next Challenge

In 1994, the Campana family moved to a big new house next to a sprawling E. & J. Gallo vineyard—essentially a fifteen-hundred-acre private park with endless biking and hiking trails under a dense canopy. Standing in my backyard, admiring my new French country mansion, I heard the distant *chop-chop* of a helicopter. Robert Gallo, chairman of the large wine company bearing his family name, was checking out his grape harvest. He circled my property to see what his new neighbor was up to, then receded until all I heard was a faint echo. I was less interested in the person aboard than the machine. What an exhilarating experience it must be to soar over the vast Central Valley, irrigation canals glinting in the sun, Sierra peaks to the east, the California Coastal Range to the west, imagining the towers of San Francisco and the Golden Gate ninety miles to the north.

What is it about the thrill of flying that attracts entrepreneurs? Does it tap into something deeper in our DNA—the lure of risk and independence? The desire to push boundaries and seek new worlds to conquer? I had always been fascinated with helicopters. Now it became an obsession. I knew one day I would own one.

Patience and moderation were never my strong suits. Not long after, I shared my not-so-secret passion with a pilot giving chopper rides at a little fair down the road. He said, "You need to call Helicopter Bruce."

I tracked Bruce Zeier to an aircraft dealership in Los Angeles and asked him over the phone, "What does a helicopter cost?"

"Are you a pilot?" he asked.

I said no, but I'd flown in one several times. He was silent for a moment, then got down to business. I might like a little Michigan-made model called the Enstrom 280FX Shark. It was easy to fly, safe, and economical—think airborne Honda Civic. He found me a used one for $200,000.

Bruce directed me to a flight instructor named Cameron Rolfe, who worked out of a general aviation airport in San Carlos, ten miles below San Francisco International. Cameron and I drove down to LA, picked up the Enstrom, and parked it in my backyard. Over the next twelve months, he introduced me to concepts like *lift*, *thrust*, and *drag*. He taught me to hover like a hummingbird, using strangely named controls like *cyclic*, *collective*, and *anti-torque pedals*. He eyed me as I ventured over my driveway and nearby tomato fields. He taught me to read dense aeronautical charts and communicate succinctly with air traffic control. Eventually, we cruised over subdivisions, looking down at the landscape I had helped shape. It was a new perspective.

After a year of reading, studying, and soaring, Cameron asked if I felt ready to take the three-part Federal Aviation Administration pilot's license exam. I took a deep breath and said sure. I aced the multiple-choice "knowledge" test but dreaded the oral quiz. As Cameron warned, the examiner grilled me on everything from engine mechanics to emergency procedures. I correctly translated codes on an aeronautical chart but was stumped when he asked me to decipher the letters *THE* over a jagged spot on the Sierras. After a painful pause, I confessed my ignorance. He smiled. "Just joking. It's the word *the*. You passed."

As we walked toward the Enstrom for the inflight test, he said, "We can do this in one of two ways. Number one, I will tell you to go in such and such a direction at such and such an altitude, and you will communicate with air traffic control. If you are not following my instructions correctly or I feel in danger, the examination is over, and you fail."

The other? "We go to McDonald's, buy a Quarter Pounder, milkshake, and fries. If you can manage all that while flying, you pass. What do you want to do?" Once again, he grinned. The kidder. "Putting you at ease. You'll do fine." And I did.

Flying gave me a bird's-eye view of the Modesto area. I saw blue specks dotting green suburban backyards. The pools symbolized the area's prosperity, the immense level of disposable income, and the new focus on lifestyle and leisure. But there were many more barren yards—unbuilt pools, potential sales. Inspired by Gerber, I had hired three salesmen to take over routine selling, three designers to create computer-aided design schematics to speed up building permits, and two schedulers to organize projects. It was a smooth-running machine. We had installed 160 pools and brought in more than six million dollars in 1995, and were sure to beat that in 1996.

But rather than resting on my laurels, sitting back and enjoying the security of success, the first thing on my mind was how to go faster.

Technology was my ally. More durable vinyl liners, improved fiberglass, and better concrete mixes reduced costs. Better excavation tools and automated systems for mixing and applying concrete made the building process faster and more efficient. Homeowners and developers recognized that pools were more than a luxury; they were investments that enhanced the value of properties.

Most of the homes going up were built by a dozen or so subdivision developers. They were typically done "on spec," without individual buyers in mind, but contracts were often in place by the time the homes were close to completion. Buyers could then modify the houses; choose from various color schemes, layouts, and finishes; and add sidewalks and patios. Why not also offer swimming pools too? That would let buyers roll the cost into their primary mortgage rather than financing them with separate home equity loans. It would make pools much more affordable, as the cost could be spread out over thirty years at a lower mortgage interest rate. Adding a pool to the first mortgage could mean adding only about a hundred dollars more to a monthly payment, making it accessible to more people.

As I eyed the sprouting subdivisions, I had another thought: Developers liked to presell homes before putting a shovel in the ground. That made it easier to get construction financing. Buyers could customize their new homes with paint, flooring, appliances, sidewalks, and patios. Why not pools? What could excite the kids more than knowing they would splash about with their friends on day one? And what could make parents happier than avoiding months of heavy construction in a brand-new backyard? Homebuyers could fold the pool into their original mortgage, meaning they could afford a bigger pool than they would using a traditional fifteen-year home improvement loan. What was not to like?

I phoned a developer I knew named Rod Lowe, and he liked the idea. We negotiated a deal giving me exclusive pre-closing rights to build pools on their properties. The lenders agreed, too—though bankers being bankers, some added caveats, such as requiring specific timelines for pool completion or placing limits on the pool cost that could be financed. Other developers saw what we were doing and soon jumped on the bandwagon. Before long, twelve were feeding me jobs. I didn't have to make sales calls, and the projects were more profitable since I didn't have to worry about competition. Homeowners often drove up prices with expensive options.

The main downside was the same one I'd encountered when selling hot tubs to pool builders twenty years earlier: I wouldn't get a penny until closing. However, the high cash flow from other projects and the company's strong balance sheet made it easy to get low-rate construction financing. Within three years, those prearranged pools accounted for half my pool projects, nearly doubling our monthly revenue by early 1999. We were averaging fifteen projects a month, ranging from simple pools to major landscaping projects. Although I kept a personal eye on every project, I had seasoned job supervisors who had risen through the ranks, knew my standards, and had my trust. On paper, my partner was the chief operating officer to whom they nominally reported, but he was often missing in action.

Where was my partner? He seemed to have completely lost interest in the business. He was supposed to oversee construction but didn't, so I dealt with site managers directly. In the early days, he'd gotten involved with a religious group called Calvary Chapel, an international association of charismatic evangelical churches, and it slowly took over his life. He spent afternoons at youth fellowship meetings or reading the Bible to prisoners. I'd ask a straightforward business question and get a long-winded response about the prodigal son, Jesus and donkeys, or Peter or Joseph. Was he intentionally being difficult, or did he think I needed educating about the meaning of life? I had no way of knowing, and eventually, I stopped caring and, for all practical purposes, moved on without him. I had enough on my plate.

Why did I let things drag on so long? I asked myself that question more often than I could count and never came up with a satisfying answer, other than that partnerships are delicate and complicated. In many ways, they're like marriages—you invest a lot, build trust over time, and when issues arise, it often feels easier to ignore them or hope they'll resolve on their own. I tend to avoid conflict, convinced I can somehow work things out without confrontation. But here, my approach meant years went by without resolution. Lynna urged me more times than I can count to bring things to a head, but I resisted.

In hindsight, I see the importance of tackling conflict early and directly. Growth and harmony sometimes require having tough conversations before resentment builds. I've learned that, even though I value collaboration, I need to push myself to address issues head-on as they arise. If I'd done that, I could have saved myself years of stress and focused on other things that mattered.

The end came when he returned from a church function in Russia during the last month of 1999. He said he wanted to move there. He knew our business relationship was nearing its end. We brought in the accountants and lawyers. I asked him what he proposed. He said nothing but wrote something on scrap paper, turned it upside down, and slid it across the conference table. It simply said "$500,000." As far as I could see, there was no rhyme or reason to it, but if that's what he wanted, so be it. I looked at him and said, "Fine, but not in a lump sum, only in installments." He nodded, and we were done.

Entrepreneurship can be isolating, and a support network is an often overlooked but crucial factor in entrepreneurial success. Building a business is tough; the emotional and mental strain can be overwhelming. Without a network, the pressure can pile up. But with strong support, you're not going it alone. The people around you can provide both practical and emotional backing, helping to sustain your energy and drive. Success is rarely a solo journey, and appreciating the role of a support network can make all the difference in staying the course.

The purpose of my life wasn't to serve my business; the purpose of my business was to serve my life. Business adversities and money problems came and went, but I would not let them undermine what Lynna and I were building.

Lynna was by my side from the early days of selling hot tubs, a steadfast companion who provided a voice of reason when I was at risk of overreaching. She grounded me when my ego clouded my judgment and offered calm during the inevitable storms. While she wasn't deeply involved in day-to-day operations, her role as a supportive partner was crucial to the company's success. Most importantly, she was our family's rock. She raised our four daughters, avoiding the dramas, drug issues, and pregnancies that plagued other families. It was no small feat, yet she did it gracefully, instilling values that helped them grow into remarkable, successful women. Education was her priority, and it became mine as well. Unhappy with Modesto's public schools, we worked diligently to ensure that all the girls received a private Catholic education. It was expensive— a sacrifice in the early days before the pool business took off—but one we never regretted.

Mindful of how my trip around the world had broadened my perspective, I valued the unique education that travel provides. As soon as we thought the girls were old enough to comprehend what they were seeing, we struck out. We wanted them to develop a love for adventure and a passion for travel. It was never easy to leave the company for two or three weeks at a time, but I lined up enough work to keep my crews busy and hit the road. I knew I'd have messes to clean up afterward, but it was a price worth paying.

We took excursions to Disneyland and Walt Disney World and hiked in Montana, Yellowstone, and the Grand Tetons. We floated down the Colorado River on rafts adapted from World War II pontoon bridges. We cooked breakfast over a fire and rode the river all day. It was quiet, with no ambient noise other than lapping water or raven calls. Then we'd see sprinkles a hundred yards ahead. A low rumble soon became a roar. Rapids ahead! How big a drop would it be? At the bottom, we looked back with awe.

We visited Paris, Rome, and the Amalfi Coast. We explored Swiss towns like Lucerne and Zermatt, where we'd ride Swiss trains. We traveled to Zermatt at the foot of the Matterhorn and took trains to Zurich and Geneva. In the Loire Valley, we visited Château de Chenonceau, which the girls remembered from a Disney TV show, and witnessed the famous dog feeding at Château de Cheverny. The girls delighted in Neuschwanstein Castle, the nineteenth-century Bavarian palace that inspired Walt Disney's *Sleeping Beauty*. People asked how I justified the cost of these excursions. I answered, "I can't afford not to. The girls are only this age once. It's my only opportunity to do it with them."

Plus, we were enjoying our new five-thousand-square-foot home, which had seven bedrooms. Each girl had one, and the older three shared a dressing room and bathroom with multiple mirrors and light fixtures like you'd find backstage at a Broadway theater. As no teenagers had cell phones at that time, we put in a phone booth for privacy. The household was female: one woman, four daughters, and one guy, browbeaten into submission. They finally agreed to a male pup, which they demanded be neutered. I could hardly complain.

During construction, I had instructed workmen to toss lumber scraps and uprooted bushes on a clearance at the bottom of a slope. By the time we moved in, the debris had risen to more than ten feet of brittle organic matter, parched by the California sun. As Lynna repeatedly pointed out, it was a fire waiting to happen. If she suspected I had a plan, she was right.

At breakfast, I announced a major event for that evening, one they wouldn't soon forget. As darkness descended, I gathered everyone outside, lit a stick of kindling, and tossed it onto the pile. Flames lit the night. The towering inferno was visible for miles on the flat Central Valley plain. The girls were delighted. Neighbors were less so. Assuming our new house was on fire, they called 911. Before long, I heard approaching sirens and the flashing red lights of Modesto fire engines and ducked into the house.

Through the window, I watched as a crew chief in full gear surveyed the situation, determined no danger, and quizzed the girls. Ten-year-old Annie pointed to the house. He looked, shook his head, got back into his truck, and roared off. I ventured outside and asked, "What did he say?" My eldest daughter rolled her eyes and looked at me sternly. "No more big fires," she said. The adult in the household.

A private life and a business life don't operate on separate tracks—they bump into each other and often overlap in surprising ways. The relationships I built with family, friends, and through community involvement helped me connect with people, shaping the way I navigated the world. Lynna and I met so many people through school, social events, and community gatherings, which helped me hone my ability to relate to others. These experiences smoothed out my rough edges, widened my perspective, and made me more empathetic—a skill that paid off when dealing with employees, suppliers, and bankers. I learned how to break down barriers that often stood in the way of communication.

Breaking down barriers became a bit of a family game. My daughters would challenge me to connect with the most stubborn people we encountered—an overly bureaucratic border guard, a mum cab driver, or an unhelpful police officer. One time, I was on an Amtrak train between Washington, DC, and New York, chaperoning one of my daughters' eighth-grade trips. The conductor was cold and distant, refusing to engage in conversation. I made it my personal mission to get him to open up. I followed him down the aisle, trying to spark a conversation. He glared at me as if I were an annoying gnat. I'm surprised he didn't order me to sit down and shut up.

By the time we reached the Hudson River, he was laughing at my puns and jokes. We were friends. At Penn Station, he pulled me into his little conductor's office and handed me a bunch of Amtrak pins for the kids. No one in my daughter's class thought I could break through, but I did.

When each of the girls was in the eighth grade, I chaperoned class trips. On one, I was elected to lead a group tour of New York City. I knew next to nothing about the city. I had no idea where we were or what we were doing. However, as was my habit in life, I decided to fake it. As the tour bus inched down Broadway, I squinted to read business signs up ahead. I'd see one for a delicatessen, press the button on the mike, and roll with it: "Coming up on the right, you'll see the famous Meyrowitz delicatessen, established in 1947 by Yasha Meyrowitz, who immigrated to this country after World War I. It has been a staple of Midtown Manhattan ever since. Look closely, and you'll spot all kinds of kosher meats hanging in the window. And on your left, you'll notice the iconic Derby restaurant, where theater actors gather after the show." I did this block by block. Everyone on that bus thought I knew what I was talking about, or at least pretended to. They were enthralled, and I gloated. A little chutzpah and showbiz improv went a long way. A useful lesson.

Community involvement expanded my social and business support network. It introduced me to potential customers in a natural, less transactional setting and helped build my reputation as a local leader. I was never the type to network just for the sake of collecting business cards. Knowing I was making a positive impact beyond my business gave me pleasure.

I was a member of the Rotary Club because I liked the idea of businesspeople coming together to make a difference. But over time, city employees, school district folks, and other government types began to dominate the meetings. I was disappointed that many of them seemed to disdain the local business community, and I gradually lost interest. The Chamber of Commerce selected me for a program called Leadership Modesto, aimed at improving community leaders' understanding of city government. I went behind the scenes of various departments, including the jails, hospitals, and sewer system. As with the Rotary Club, it seemed a better idea in theory than in actuality, and I moved on. There was too much of what we now call "virtue signaling" and too little action.

Still, interacting with people outside the construction orbit enhanced my social and interpersonal skills, which are among the most underrated qualities in business. Money may be the goal and a customary measure of success, but business is fundamentally about people. As bumper stickers say: "It's the journey, not the destination." And the journey is mostly a series of interactions with other people.

As I approached my fiftieth birthday, I recalled Zig Ziglar's words, reiterated in his 1982 book, *Secrets of Closing the Sale*: "You can have everything in life you want if you will just help other people get what they want." I thought about the people who had influenced me: Steve Marchette, who showed me the world; Uncle Nick, who gave me an early education on the streets of San Francisco; my dad, who instilled a solid work ethic in me; and Barden Stevenot, who saw potential in a young man with ambition but little direction. Where would I be without those people?

I felt a strong drive to pay it forward.

One of my crew supervisors, a young man named Craig Whitcomb, always had something extra. He knew how to motivate workers and address myriad construction issues without losing his cool. I sensed that he could go far—he even could have taken over Vintage one day. He approached me with a request. After we finished constructing a pool, there was a critical embryonic period where the water chemistry needed to be balanced to prevent the walls from staining. This two-to-three-week phase required regular adjustments to pH and other chemical levels.

Craig wanted to start a side business on weekends to provide this service. I agreed, happy to support his enterprising spirit. I could have done this in-house, as pool maintenance could provide steady residual income and often led to additional work like pump upgrades or repairs. But I let Craig take it on. He built a successful business, with routes of thirty or forty pools. The pools we built were often clustered in neighborhoods due to referrals, so Craig's routes were efficient, and he could easily handle them in his off-hours.

Over time, Craig realized he could make more money building up routes and selling them than doing the actual servicing. A $100 monthly maintenance account could fetch $800. Since we were building four hundred pools yearly, and about 40 percent of those clients signed up for Craig's maintenance service, he built a nice business flipping routes.

Craig also started a little business with his uncle, installing baby barriers around pools. He eventually asked if I would sign state paperwork to help him get his California swimming pool contractor's license. I was happy to do it, seeing how far he had come. Remembering those who inspired, encouraged, and bailed me out when I was on the edge, I was thankful I had the opportunity to pay something forward.

When Helicopter Bruce phoned me in early 2000 about a used Hughes 369 helicopter that became available, I couldn't get it out of my mind. There was nothing wrong with my practical Enstrom, but the 369 was in another league—a Porsche 911 versus a Toyota Camry. Socrates supposedly said, "He who is not content with what he has would not be content with what he would like to have." Or something to that effect. Maybe so, but I was willing to take that chance.

The 369, a civilian version of the Hughes OH-6 Cayuse, was a single-engine light helicopter designed and produced by Howard Hughes's company for the US Army. The Army used more than a thousand in Vietnam, often to flush out enemy antiaircraft positions. It later became a mainstay of police aviation units. The LAPD pursued O. J. Simpson's white Bronco in one. Powered by a jet turbine rather than pistons, it was fast, agile, and sleek. I had to have one.

The 369, formerly owned by the San Bernardino Sheriff's Department, was priced at $350,000. "It's the best deal you're going to get on one of these things," he said. When we picked it up in Janesville, Wisconsin, I spotted what looked like two bullet holes near the engine compartment. The seller said they dated to Vietnam. The Army replaced the working parts, but the holes remained. I opened the clamshell door and saw no sign of damage. The war wounds added another layer of mystique.

We took turns flying back to Modesto, skimming five hundred feet over Mississippi River barges, Kansas cornfields, and small-town cemeteries. We navigated southwest to avoid the Rockies, stopping at self-service aviation pumps every three or four hours and spending nights in inexpensive motels. Zipping over high plains grasslands and shrub-dotted deserts at 150 miles an hour, we encountered occasional destabilizing dips called *arroyos*. They felt like roller coaster free falls, momentarily taking my breath away and jerking me out of reverie.

There's a saying that the most intense living happens when you're skimming the edge of death. I wasn't trying to crash and burn, but the possibility was there. This wasn't about fear; it was about staying so sharp you could shave with your own nerves. Flying demanded hard-nosed discipline. There was no room for bluff, no room for second chances. You either knew what to do, or you didn't. You learned how to land an engine-out mess of a plane, or you took a nosedive trying. One slip could make you a permanent statistic. That was the charge— the kind of energy that makes life taste like blood and salt.

A military controller radioed permission to overfly restricted airspace at Kirtland Air Force Base, near Albuquerque. "Enjoy the show," he said. We didn't understand what he meant until four F-15s roared by so closely that we could see our reflections in the pilots' visors. On day three, we traced Highway 99, slicing through the flat, endless Central Valley. When we finally dropped onto my backyard landing pad, I was bone-tired but crackling with energy, like I'd outrun the devil. It was the kind of charge I'd felt setting off around the world and in the frantic early days of hot tubs and pools. I missed that and wanted more of it.

The speed and long range of the 369 offered unparalleled convenience. I could step out my back door and reach the Sierra foothills in twenty-five minutes. I was fifty miles from the Pacific Ocean, eighty miles from Yosemite, and one hundred miles from Lake Tahoe. A round trip by car would take a day. The helicopter could take me there for lunch.

A drive from the Central Valley to San Francisco International was a gnarly two-and-a-half-hour journey. Lynna and I flew to nearby San Carlos in twenty-five minutes and took a ten-minute car ride to the main terminal. Admittedly, this level of convenience was a rare luxury. Obtaining a pilot's license and buying, maintaining, and refueling the aircraft was not economically sensible. However, the psychic rewards were priceless.

The Hughes may have looked like a Porsche, but it felt like a Humvee. With four rotor blades and a jet-powered engine, it climbed fast and cruised like a peregrine falcon over the Central Valley landscape. It was crazy fun to pilot, but the engine was so loud that passengers had to wear headphones over earplugs, which was hardly conducive to conversation. As a social person, I envisioned family outings in the air and bonding experiences with friends and neighbors; instead, we retreated into our little worlds.

Jet turbines had a limited lifespan. The 369 needed a complete rebuild at around four thousand flight hours, a $325,000 job. Ouch. After three years of ownership, mine was seventy hours short of that. I sold it for $170,000 to a guy willing to invest in it. He considered it a good deal, as he could sell the refurbished helicopter for at least $700,000. I was more than ready to move on—in more ways than one.

The life cycle of a small business resembles that of fruit: It gets pollinated, matures, ripens, and eventually rots. I didn't want to see The Vintage Company reach that final stage. So, in early 2004, I quietly put out word that it was for sale. There was no need to spook clients or send employees into a frenzy. And the last thing I wanted was some bargain hunter sniffing around, thinking he could pick up a "distressed asset" for pennies. Better to keep the ship steady and let the sharks circle on my terms. Despite the headaches, it was a valuable asset, arguably the strongest pool-building and landscape-design firm in the Central Valley. I had assembled a system that no one could easily replicate. It had a reputation for excellent customer service. The crews were well trained. It had the most extensive fleet of dump trucks, excavators, and other equipment in good working order. The exclusive contracts with Modesto's subdivision contractors were cherries on the cake.

Richard Townsend, the owner of Aqua Pool and Spa, phoned. I knew him only slightly but couldn't have been happier to hear from him, as he was one of the few competitors with the financial resources to buy me out. "Maybe we should talk," he said. Two months later, we signed the papers. *Here you go, boy*, I thought. *Take it and run.* Four years later, after the 2008 fiscal crisis, I heard rumors that the company had gone belly-up but didn't bother to check them out. My mind was on the future.

## Entrepreneurial Life Lessons

- When issues arise, it often feels easier to ignore them or hope they'll resolve on their own. They won't.

- The entrepreneurial journey is a series of interactions with other people.

- The life cycle of a small business resembles that of fruit: It gets pollinated, matures, ripens, and eventually rots.

- The entrepreneur who knows himself also knows when to exit.

# 8

# Interlude

## Evaluating Options

After selling their companies, successful business owners often find themselves bored and twitchy. They've spent years in the trenches, building up their empires, only to wake up one morning with no fires to put out, no deals to chase, and nothing but time on their hands. It's like going from a war zone to a knitting circle. That sense of accomplishment fades faster than they'd like to admit. Without urgent goals or fires to douse, a strange void opens up, and suddenly they're staring down frustration, even a touch of depression. With no structure or sense of purpose, they're left scrambling to reinvent themselves. And without a clear second act, they can feel like a captain lost at sea, clinging to a navigation chart that no longer makes sense.

I could relate. I wanted more and was searching for something to challenge me. I wanted to feel that excitement again—the risk and thrill that motivated me in the beginning and that I felt gripping the cyclic of the 369.

Fortunately, I had more options than most entrepreneurs. While building the pool business, I had also developed a couple of side gigs. One was in residential real estate, where I invested in and built speculative houses. Another was a wedding banquet business that I started in an old building I had acquired years earlier for storing pool construction supplies but could no longer use for that purpose due to zoning regulations (more about that in the next chapter). In addition to those two ventures, I also had an idea for a third business aimed at helping other entrepreneurs sell their companies. I always had multiple projects going at once; I couldn't focus on just one. I don't know if that's a scattered personality or what, but I needed creative outlets.

I had gotten into real estate early in my pool-building days. It wasn't exactly something I needed, what with a new marriage, a chaotic schedule, and a precarious financial situation. But practicalities never stood in my way. I saw an opportunity and grabbed it. My timing could have been better; I nearly lost my shirt. But I learned enough to eventually make it a profitable calling, so it was a useful education.

Driving around new housing developments on pool sales calls in early 1981, I had noticed that most contractors were selling spec houses with all the appeal of a prison yard. The yards were empty; they just raked the dirt and added a concrete walkway to the front door. Inside, the homes were bare and cheap looking, considering the high prices. In my mind, the developers were penny-wise and pound-foolish. They were leaving money on the table. There was so much they could do to make the homes more attractive, sell them faster, and increase their profits. I would show them how to do it right and offer a fully finished product, with upgraded kitchens and bathrooms, a nicely landscaped yard, and, to top it off, a swimming pool. It would be a dream home, with a price to match.

I asked Lynna how she'd feel about me using some of the income from the pool business to do it. The pool business generated a lot of cash, so I could pay for supplies and labor as I went along. With her buy-in, I bought a development lot near the country club and started construction.

Unfortunately, by the time the beautifully landscaped home hit the market in the spring of 1982, the country had entered a deep recession. Unemployment was high, and interest rates were off the charts. I knew I would be lucky to get anywhere close to the $600,000 I had invested. That was a massive price tag at that time. Nineteen houses were for sale on the same street alone, and nobody was buying. It was a tight spot.

There I was, mowing the lawn, when Fran pulled up—owner of the nursery where I'd bought enough plants and lawn supplies to create my own rainforest. She'd been keeping tabs on my project, dropping by on weekends to check it out. "I'm interested in your house," she said, leaning out the car window. "How much do you want?" I gave her the number: $650,000. She gave me a raised eyebrow and a nod—classic poker face. A week later, she was back. "Five hundred thousand," she said flatly. "Take it or leave it." She knew I was in a bind and thought she'd found a soft spot.

I laughed—not sure if from nerves or disbelief. If Fran was really after a deal, she'd be haggling with someone else by now, not low-balling me on my front lawn. I said, "Fran, if $500,000's the best I can get, I'll move in myself and let my kids redecorate with crayons." She looked as if I'd slapped her with a cactus—insulted, wounded pride and all. No deal, or so I thought. Two days later, she was back: "Fine. I'll buy your house for $650,000."

The lesson? Trusting my instincts paid off. I didn't need to undersell myself. If I built something people really wanted, they'd find a way to pay for it. I realized I could set myself apart by creating properties that had real pull—places with landscaping, pools, and finishes that made a great first impression.

Another takeaway? Forget hiring a real estate agent—I'd handle sales myself. I figured I could sell better than 95 percent of the agents out there, and there's nothing like selling your own product to convey confidence. Upscale buyers—doctors, lawyers, and the like—appreciated the direct approach and the fact that the homes were ready to move in.

Building pools for Modesto's well-to-do introduced me to the area's top developers and contractors—a breed with a few common traits. They could smell where the real estate market was going, knew how to jump on an opportunity early, and needed capital to pull it off.

One day, while digging out a pool in the backyard of a general contractor named Rick, he walked me through his latest idea: Investors he knew had bought raw land near a country club, rezoned it from agricultural to residential, and flipped the lots for a killing. Rick figured he could build a home on one for under $400,000 and sell it for $750,000. Problem was, he didn't have the financing to back the project. I mulled it over. Vintage was bringing in over $900,000 a month—more than enough to scrape off a little for an investment without feeling the pinch. A few days later, I called Rick and said I was game. He gave me two options: We could either partner, or I could buy the lot outright and hire him to build. Having learned my lesson with partnerships, I took the latter.

Rick was a talented builder who knew his way around a job site. He took care of the foundation and framing, brought in subcontractors for electrical and plumbing, and left the interior to me. After years of visiting homes while selling pools, I was convinced I could design as well as anyone with a degree. I chose the granite, cabinets, tile, and designed a matching pool with landscaping to boot. Eighteen months later, the house sold fast, and I pocketed $125,000. Over the next decade, Rick and I built seven custom homes together—enough extra cash to put my kids through college.

I had no interest in constructing bespoke houses for specific clients. Two months on a custom pool was already a test of patience. I'd seen other building contractors wrestle with clients who'd turn every decision—tile, cabinet handles, paint color—into a life-and-death crisis, and I wanted none of it. I liked to finish the house exactly as I wanted, put it up for sale, and move on. If someone had an issue with the granite or light fixtures, they could rip them out or buy something else.

As side hustles go, real estate was profitable and not too much of a headache, though I knew I'd never devote my life to it. It was a good way to make money, but hardly a calling.

The news was everywhere: Millions of aging baby boomer entrepreneurs, like me, were putting their businesses on the block. Their overindulged kids either didn't want the responsibility or couldn't tell a balance sheet from a grocery list. As a seasoned entrepreneur, I got it—I understood both sides of the table. And hearing about all these owners in my generation scrambling to pass the baton to a generation that couldn't care less got me thinking. I wanted to dig into what makes sellers tick, how buyers and investors size things up, and what lenders want to see. Plus, I wanted to crack the code on properly valuing a business.

So, I set my sights on becoming a Certified Business Intermediary (CBI). Think of a CBI as a real estate broker who swaps small businesses instead of houses. They handle it all—valuations, negotiations, everything short of packing boxes for the new owners. And somewhere in the back of my mind was the thought that being a business broker might let me spot companies worth snapping up myself.

I quickly learned that selling a company makes selling a house look like child's play. Buyers can't just wander through, kick the tires, or spot-check for mold in the basement. A business is a pile of spreadsheets and projections, all bundled up with a little hope and a lot of guesswork. How do you even put a price tag on that? Sure, it might be raking in profit today, but take away the founder's cozy handshake deals with suppliers and loyal customers and what's left? Is the industry thriving or nose-diving? A smart buyer will ask all these questions, and the seller needs answers. That's where the middleman comes in, as the "honest broker" who crunches numbers, flags red flags, and wrangles lawyers and accountants to bring it all home.

So I threw myself into the world of business brokerage, devouring courses from the International Business Brokers Association on everything from valuations and deal structures to tax rules and financial deep dives. There was even a tough exam to pass, but I plowed through it all in six months instead of the usual two years. My experience running a business helped, but there was still plenty to pick up—negotiating, financing, the works. And after those six months, I was an official CBI.

Whatever rosy notions I'd had about business brokering vanished fast. Business sales were a minefield of ego, emotion, and headache—leagues beyond real estate. Sellers who'd poured years into their businesses were often convinced they were sitting on Fort Knox and would inflate the asking price until the whole thing imploded. Others were so desperate they'd practically take anything to walk away. Buyers, on the other hand, loved sniffing out excuses to lowball—a profit margin a hair below average, a weird blip in last year's sales, you name it. The smart ones dug beyond the spreadsheets to ask why the owner wants out, because nine times out of ten, if a seller can't give a straight answer, they're ditching a sinking ship.

Adding a layer of complexity, most buyers rely on loans, often backed by the Small Business Administration. Lenders don't just glance at balance sheets; they dive into cash flow and pore over monthly checking accounts looking for red flags. Lenders also size up the buyer's collateral, credit, and experience, not to mention industry risk factors.

Even if a deal survives all that scrutiny, there's still a good chance it will unravel. I've seen them fall apart when a seller got cold feet at the eleventh hour. Identities get tangled up in the businesses, or founders panic at the thought of living off a lump sum.

Fewer than 30 percent of businesses that hit the market actually sell. I decided life was too short for this particular rodeo.

My back-of-the-mind idea to use the proceeds from the pool and landscaping company deal to buy, fix, and flip businesses looked like a better bet—though still a long shot. The catch? Most businesses for sale were gasping for air—owners desperate to dump their headaches on the next poor soul. But sometimes a headache has hidden potential if you squint at it the right way. A struggling business in a good market can be worth its weight in licenses, leases, equipment, and infrastructure alone. Often, the problem isn't what they're selling—it's how they're running it. Strategy, management, finances—you name it, there's usually room for improvement, or at least a place to start.

First, I needed to find a short list of "fixable" businesses. That's where I stumbled upon an unexpected ally: the US government. I'm normally skeptical of anything the federal government does. I agree with what Ronald Reagan said: "The nine most terrifying words in the English language are: I'm from the government, and I'm here to help." In this case, I was impressed. The Commerce Department had this massive database that classified every business under the sun with Standard Industrial Classification (SIC) codes. These four-digit codes let you slice and dice industries to see how one company stacks up against its competitors and trends, valuations, and market dynamics. In other words, the SIC is kind of a cheat sheet for spotting underachievers and high-fliers.

While digging into SIC data, I noticed something curious: In nearly every industry, a few businesses stood out, head and shoulders above the rest. They weren't just skating by on luck—they were running laps around the competition. I'd known owners like that over the years: people who simply got it, who optimized every process and took inefficiency out back and shot it. Seeing it on paper only confirmed what I'd always suspected—success was about capitalizing on what others missed. This data-backed realization underscored why focusing on the right improvements could turn a mediocre business into a moneymaker.

Enter Discount Plumbing, a small-time operation in Manteca, in nearby San Joaquin County. The owner, a guy in his late fifties, approached me to see if I'd help him sell it. Looking at the books, though, I doubted anyone would want it. While other plumbing outfits were cashing in, Discount was treading water. What was the issue? Even a faltering business can have value; it just depends where you look.

I brought in Kyle Weinheimer, a finance whiz and former classmate of my daughter Annie. Kyle sifted through the numbers and came back with a mixed review: "It's broken," he said, "but I think we can fix it."

The core issue? Discount was using an outdated hourly billing model, which made customers price shop and look elsewhere. More successful plumbing outfits had moved to a flat-rate pricing system, so customers would know up front exactly what they'd pay. Instead of billing $150 an hour to unclog a drain, they charged a flat $225. The job could take five minutes or five hours, but either way, the customer wasn't left sweating the clock.

I went back to Discount's owner and told him I was interested in buying in. Naturally, he gave me a suspicious look. I'd initially said the business wasn't worth selling, and now I was making an offer. Was I trying to hustle him? I explained Kyle's flat-rate model idea. The owner knew about it; he just didn't want the hassle of overhauling his system, much less the costs of new software and hardware. But with some back-and-forth, I convinced him it was the only way the business had a shot. In the end, I secured a 75 percent stake, and Discount Plumbing was in for a major overhaul.

Kyle took the reins on rolling out the new flat-rate system. We hired a software outfit called Northstar Automation to set us up with a program that had more bells and whistles than a carnival. It took nearly a year of hand-holding and hairpulling to get the thing running smoothly. Northstar's database came stocked with prices for more than three thousand plumbing tasks, from unclogging toilets to installing water heaters and replacing sewer lines. Each task came with a built-in commission: A plumber could pocket $135 for a water heater install, no matter how fast they wrapped it up. The incentive? Work quicker, make the same cash, and skip the nickel-and-diming with customers.

It wasn't exactly a smooth transition. Plenty of plumbers looked at the system like it was written in hieroglyphics. Two dozen either quit or were shown the door before we had a solid crew who "got it." But once we did, the whole operation turned highly profitable. The effective hourly rate went from $150 to $375, and plumbers stopped watching the clock and started watching their bank balances.

In the grand scheme, Kyle was the brains, I was the moneyman, and without both of us, this whole deal would've gone nowhere. After four years, I backed away and left Kyle in charge. Truth be told, I was bored. Running things day-to-day just isn't my game. I like building and fixing. Once that's done, my eyes start to glaze over. I needed a fresh challenge to sink my teeth into, so I moved on, leaving Kyle to keep the place running.

Not long after, the founder decided he wanted a piece of his old business back, so I sold my share, leaving Kyle and him to keep things going. Kyle funneled his earnings into law school and, after the original owner passed away, ended up owning the company outright—now valued in the millions. Not bad for a plumbing outfit that once couldn't tell a flat rate from a flat tire.

At Heli-Expo (now Verticon) in Los Angeles, March 2003, a gleaming Bell 206B JetRanger turbine caught my eye. It wasn't as quick or nimble as the Hughes 369, but it had practicality stamped all over it, a family machine. Five passengers, luxury seating, quiet enough for a conversation that didn't involve shouting, and big, curved windows to soak up the view—it was like the helicopter version of a first-class upgrade. After selling the Hughes, the JetRanger set me back $180,000. I swapped a Porsche for a Suburban.

Among other things, it meant I could fly my daughter Katrina up to the University of Oregon in Eugene—a quick three-hour hop with one refuel. That beat a nine-hour drive, and I pictured us having one of those father–daughter bonding trips, a mini adventure filled with heart-to-hearts at 4,500 feet. In reality? Let's just say it wasn't quite like the movie in my head. Flying a helicopter is an exercise in focus: no autopilot, no space to drift off, no "highway hypnosis." Katrina wasn't exactly thrilled either. What twenty-year-old wants hours of small talk with her dad? And the return trip alone was . . . well, about as exciting as you'd expect.

At some point, I started to wonder what had possessed me to buy such an extravagant toy. The passenger seats usually sat empty. Friends and family had schedules that didn't include bopping around in a chopper. Mostly, it was me and one other person or, more often, just me—airborne and alone. With my daughters slowly peeling off to college, the JetRanger was looking like a sad mistake. So I put it on the market, hoping the next owner would have richer experiences.

In 2012, when my youngest daughter, Caroline, enrolled at Boise State, 650 miles away, we flew commercial, and it sucked. Driving to San Francisco and catching a Southwest flight to Boise was a drudge. I perked up when a local businessman named Don Monaco put his Beechcraft V-tail Bonanza airplane on the market. I got out my checkbook.

At least part of the thrill was the chance to meet Monaco. At seventy-five, he was a Central Valley legend, a successful businessman, promoter, and guerrilla marketer known for riding a gas-powered skateboard down J Street every Fourth of July.

More impressive, he was a dauntless aviator who flew a single-engine plane from California to Paris. He owned a World War II T-6 trainer with an eight-hundred-horsepower radial engine that could go straight up. At air shows he did "hammerheads," aerobatic maneuvers where an airplane climbs vertically until nearly stopping in midair, pivots 180 degrees, and dives straight down as the crowd gasps. He also financed Lakesters, race cars that set land speed records at Bonneville Salt Flats. I wanted to get to know him.

I phoned and told him I was interested in the Bonanza. We met at his private hangar, a museum of race cars, trophies, and other memorabilia. He walked me over to the craft he was selling. It was a four-seater that pilots called a "slick" airplane because its retractable landing gear enabled it to cruise at 175 miles an hour. The model had earned an unfortunate moniker as the "forked-tail doctor killer" because of several fatal crashes at the hands of wealthy amateur pilots. Donnie winced when I said that, saying the slur was unfair. "In the hands of a good pilot, it's as safe as any other private plane," he said. Why was he selling? Insurance reasons. Underwriters were nervous about his age.

The plane was a beauty. We shook on the spot.

One problem: I couldn't legally fly it. I had a helicopter license, but I needed a fixed-wing permit, which could take months to get. Donnie—that's what he said I should call him—handed me a key to the hangar and said I could keep the plane there as long as necessary; I could come and go as I pleased. As we parted, I thought of Humphrey Bogart strolling with Claude Rains at the end of *Casablanca*, the Lockheed Electra bearing Ingrid Bergman taking off into the foggy night. "I think," said Bogie, "this is the beginning of a beautiful friendship." In my mind, Donnie and I had a special bond.

How would I use my quarter-million-dollar impulse purchase? Other than the Boise trips, I had no clue. Most of my work was within twenty-five miles of Modesto, so I couldn't justify it as a business expense. Still, I was determined to master the sleek beast. Flying an airplane was not that difficult, especially for someone who flew helicopters. Most people go the other way: They fly an airplane and then decide to fly a helicopter because it's more complex. Getting the license wasn't difficult either, just time consuming. I hired an instructor to help me get a fixed-wing license and teach me the Beechcraft's peculiarities. As a helicopter pilot, I knew how to run the radios and was familiar with Federal Aviation Administration rules and protocols. Within six months, I was soloing over the Central Valley in the Bonanza.

Caroline and I got up at six on Mondays, drove to the Modesto airport, and breakfasted in Boise before nine. I picked her up after Friday classes. Lynna and I took day trips with friends to Las Vegas, Palm Springs, and Lake Tahoe, as well as longer excursions to Montana and Arizona. The Western United States was our backyard.

It was fun while it lasted. In 2019, Lynna was returning from Ireland, where Katrina was living with her husband, Lino Mansoni, who was awaiting his US green card. I was preparing to fly the Bonanza to San Carlos Airport, near San Francisco, where general aviation planes could land. Lynna would taxi from San Francisco International to San Carlos, and we'd fly back to Modesto. It would take us twenty minutes to get home versus a three-hour drive.

I wheeled the Bonanza out of the hangar onto the ramp and hit the starter. Nothing. The battery was dead. I connected ground power cables to jump-start the engine, not realizing I had left the ignition on. The propellers started spinning before I could reach the cockpit to cut the engine. The Bonanza rolled down the ramp, hit a car, and crashed into a fence. In three seconds, my beautiful airplane became a worthless heap of junk. It was terrifying and depressing. The only saving grace was that it hit a car, which kept it from crashing into a nearby office building, possibly causing fatalities. I looked at the wreckage, thankful that the plane was fully insured, but I decided it was an omen. I threw the insurance money in the bank and, at age sixty-five, figured my flying days were over.

## Entrepreneurial Life Lessons

- Retired business owners can face boredom, even depression, unless they find a new mission.

- Most businesses for sale are struggling—owners desperate to pass on their headaches to the next poor soul.

- A mediocre business can contain the seeds of a money-maker if a buyer knows where to look.

# 9

# The Redwood Café

## Finding the Hidden Gem

The path to success rarely runs straight. Sometimes, what looked like a dead end or a modest side gig transforms into something significant. Ambitious entrepreneurs are flexible and alert to opportunities, both within and beyond their familiar territories. Skills acquired in one endeavor are often transferable, and indeed, bringing a fresh perspective to another industry can catapult a new entrant to the front of the pack.

For me, such an opportunity hid in plain sight, and my daughters had to point it out. They nudged me with hints, suggestions, and pleas until I finally recognized it. Had it not been for their foresight, my subsequent life and career would have turned out far differently.

Vintage Gardens was a wedding and banquet venue I had owned for fifteen years. In 1994, my partner and I bought a small plot on the northern edge of town—1.8 acres surrounded by farmland and weeds—to store equipment, but zoning laws dashed that plan. His sister, my old flame, suggested opening a wedding venue since the area was zoned for food and liquor service.

The wedding and banquet business boomed, and we'd be booked months in advance. The only hitch was that weddings were a weekend business; the kitchen and dining room sat empty five or six days a week. Why not expand into a full-service restaurant to fill those tables daily and get more mileage out of that expensive commercial kitchen? The *Modesto Bee* was enthusiastic and ran a glowing feature about us, our smiling faces gracing the page. The article told of a plan to open a second location downtown. "It's going to be an absolute dream," the writer concluded. I thought I had the Midas touch. People I barely knew would gush, "You're so good, so smart, so successful!" I looked in the mirror and saw a mover and shaker, someone who had cracked the code.

Albert Einstein supposedly observed that the only thing more dangerous than ignorance is arrogance. Whether or not he actually said that, it was certainly true in my case. Looking back, I marvel at how naive I'd been. I had assumed that my success in the construction business was evidence of intuitive business genius. What I failed to grasp was that different businesses require different skills. Sure, some things are transferable—knowledge of finance and knowing how to manage people are portable—but each industry is different in its own way. The restaurant game wasn't like the pool construction game.

Construction was more forgiving. I made money when I sold the project, and hefty deposits at the start of each phase locked in profits. Even when I made mistakes, I had a cushion. On a $40,000 pool, I could have a $15,000 profit—that covered a lot of errors.

Restaurant margins were razor thin. We had to open the doors daily and pay chefs, cooks, waiters, busboys, and dishwashers without knowing if a single customer would come in. The fridge was stocked with food that would go bad if it didn't sell. My electricity bill tripled. Weekends were chaotic as I tried to juggle wedding guests with restaurant customers. Customers were quick to judge and even quicker to complain if something went wrong. Attracting patrons was tough, too. The decor was makeshift—just tables, chairs, and tablecloths thrown together. It looked like an afterthought, and honestly, it was. Disappearing food and liquor was another problem. A waiter would tell customers "The house wants to buy you dessert tonight" to get a bigger tip. A dishwasher put steaks in garbage bags, tossed them in the dumpster, and returned after closing to retrieve them. I only noticed missing inventory much later, and by then it was too late.

After eight months of losses, I shut down the ill-advised restaurant before it burned a bigger hole in my bank account. It didn't ruin me financially, but the money I threw into it could've gone into savings instead of disappearing into a pit. That mistake taught me a lot. It grounded me and reminded me that the world doesn't bend to my will. At least I had the sense to swallow my pride and cut my losses.

Returning to weddings and banquets restored Vintage Gardens to profitability. By the time I sold the pool business, the venue hosted thirty to fifty weddings each year, generating between $400,000 and $700,000 annually. The business coasted on inertia while I had my plate full of CBI and helicopters.

When the 2008 fiscal crisis put a damper on weddings, I briefly toyed with the idea of selling Vintage Gardens. My daughter Katrina, perhaps worried idle hands were the devil's workshop, said, "Why don't you open another restaurant? Things are different now." The area around Dale Avenue and Bangs Street, home to Vintage Gardens, had shifted dramatically from a quiet, semi-industrial zone with a scattering of warehouses and open lots to a busy corridor of new development. Retail centers, office complexes, and new housing pointed to ongoing expansion. With the opening of the Kaiser Permanente Modesto Medical Center just across the street, thousands of patients, staff, and visitors flowed through the area daily.

"Okay," I said reluctantly. "Let me think about it." I had learned the hard way that restaurants can be money pits for people with too much ego and too little common sense. Friends cautioned me not to reenter the business because of the high failure rate. And that was true; restaurants did have a high failure rate, even more than other start-ups. To understand why, I dove into the business side of the industry. From articles and industry reports, I gained insight into the critical role of marketing, location, and consistent service quality. My background as a Certified Business Intermediary gave me the tools to analyze financials. I examined management practices, learning how successful owners monitor food costs, control inventory, and handle fluctuating profit margins.

My own experience managing a service-based business highlighted the necessity of having a solid, strategic foundation. It became clear to me that relying solely on enthusiasm, without a strong grounding in business fundamentals, is a recipe for failure. This information and these tools led me to conclude that restaurants weren't inherently riskier than other businesses; it was that people who start restaurants rarely understand business.

Although the restaurant would use the same physical facility as the wedding business, I did not want to call it, as some suggested, The Vintage Gardens Café. Even after fifteen years, memories of that flop burned in my mind. After kicking around several other monikers, I settled on the Redwood Café, because it reminded me of my youth in the Sierras. It also evoked the grandeur and natural beauty of California's iconic redwood forests and cultural heritage and suggested a warm, inviting atmosphere.

The building needed a lot of work to get up to snuff and up to code. Banquets and weddings were held in gardens under the California sun, and food was served in tents. But restaurant patrons wanted a different experience. It would be a big investment.

My partner was another complication. Although he was long out of my life—other than the monthly $5,000 checks I was still sending him as part of the breakup settlement—he still owned half the property, which wasn't part of that deal. I was more likely to win Powerball than wrestle money out of him to pay for the cost of upgrading the facility. I offered to buy him out for another $380,000. He dickered through his lawyer and agreed after a month of international back-and-forth. When we agreed on a price, he refused to fly from Moscow to sign the papers, forcing us to do it through the American Embassy. A final aggravation.

On day one, I thought, *What kind of restaurant should I start?* I had heard you made money on the bar, so I got a liquor license. Then I had to figure out wine and food pairings. And how formal should it be? Americans didn't want to dress up for anything, especially in Middle America. I wanted a balance. When people came in, I wanted them to feel relaxed and welcome—no pretenses. But at the same time, if you wanted to order a $500 bottle of wine, you could. That balance set the tone of the place. The service had to be friendly, laid-back, but still attentive. People wanted good food, good wine, great cocktails. And I thought of it like a country club. After golf, people casually hang out in the bar. But when it's dinner time, they dress up a bit by wearing slacks or a casual dress.

The fine-casual destination restaurant that I envisioned needed a wine cellar, and the only place to put one was in a spidery dungeon that could only hold a few bottles, assuming you could persuade a steward to go down there. I made a deal with a church pastor to whom the courts sent convicted minor drug offenders as an alternative to jail. He brought in a flock of fifty potential inmates who jackhammered out the basement floor and carried it out in five-gallon buckets. We repoured the floor with concrete to create a beautiful wine cellar that we stocked with about $150,000 worth of wine. I didn't miss the irony of paying recovering addicts to build a temple of booze, but as far as I was concerned, they were both noble causes.

Businesses need room to grow organically. Push too hard, and you'll make strategic mistakes you'll later regret. You have to take time to tweak your formula, refine your systems, build your team, and connect with customers. That was easy enough to say during the day but harder to reckon with at 3 a.m. when visions of laid-off employees, shuttered doors, and embarrassed glances from old friends swirled. "Build it and they will come" was a great movie line but of little comfort when half the tables were empty at 8 p.m. on Saturday.

I considered my lack of restaurant experience an advantage, not a detriment; a strength, not a weakness. I remembered Michael Gerber's admonition in *The E-Myth* that successful entrepreneurs worked on the business, not in it. I took his warning that restaurant owners needed to stay out of the kitchen literally, not just metaphorically. I also recalled Robert Kiyosaki's *Rich Dad, Poor Dad* advice about the importance of delegating effectively, building systems, and focusing on high-value activities. I used *The Goal*'s idea of breaking work into its simplest parts: The busser would just bus tables. The server would take care of the customers. The hostess would greet folks at the door. The chef would handle the food, the line cook would work the grill, and the dishwasher would stay in the back, washing dishes. Each job was segmented just right, based on the skills needed. That way, every position did its part well.

In the same way that Tom Hopkins's tapes were my sales bible, Danny Meyer's book *Setting the Table: The Transforming Power of Hospitality in Business* was my guidebook. His first restaurant, New York City's Union Square Café, was a resounding success, as were several later ventures. His blueprint for a successful business focused less on culinary excellence and more on hospitality and relationships. Consistency and mastery of detail were critical. Customers didn't like surprises; they valued predictability. It was a model I would emulate.

Meyer's restaurant management formula revolved around the concept of "enlightened hospitality"—prioritizing the well-being of employees first, followed by customers, community, suppliers, and investors. His philosophy was that taking care of staff created a ripple effect, fostering a positive environment that enhanced the overall guest experience. The first and most important foundation of hospitality is to make sure your team members feel they are number one in your life. If you're taking good care of your employees, they'll take good care of the guests.

How did I want customers to feel when they first walked in? When they left two hours later? I saw the restaurant experience as a mini journey, like a great movie or book. People would come to the Redwood Café to celebrate birthdays and anniversaries or entertain out-of-town guests. They wanted to kindle or sustain romance, escape the humdrum, and forget their troubles. My job was to help.

I imagined the vibe of stepping in the door on a warm Modesto evening: a refreshing draft of cool air, the soft chatter of a welcoming crowd. Research told me that smell triggered memory fifty times more than sight—who forgot the aroma of Grandma's cookies?—so I bought an expensive scent machine from a New York company. I obsessed over decor, lighting, shadows, and traffic flow. I selected tableware, sat in every chair, and chose the background music. How did I do this without seeming staged or phony? I had only my gut and the unerring sensibility of my wife.

If I had learned anything in the pool business, it was that a company was not a one-man show. Micromanaging wouldn't work, even if my nerves could handle it. A successful enterprise needed a system and a team to keep it running. It took me a long time to build a system and team in the pool business. There was no excuse for not focusing on that from the beginning. I sought managers who understood job segmentation, prioritized efficiency, and knew how to build and motivate teams. Fortunately, I found Lorna Borges and Gerry Carter to run the show jointly. Lorna started at Vintage Gardens when it opened, doing weddings, banquets, and a little bookkeeping. Everyone loved her. She was easygoing and quick to take on any task or solve any problem. I depended on her to manage my life and keep me sane. Gerry was a restaurant man his whole life—two years here, three years there. He knew more about food and wine than anyone else in the Central Valley restaurant business. His easygoing personality attracted talent and created a collegial atmosphere. He looked like he was not doing anything but got everything done.

In pool building, I knew talent often lurked in unexpected places, so I was committed to nurturing it and serving as a mentor when the opportunity arose, paying it forward. One day, a wiry, sunburned young man walked into the restaurant and politely asked to speak with the manager. He seemed nervous and tentative. He said his name was Danny Tabera, and he was just out of the Marines and needed a job. Gerry hired him to bus tables. Danny and I chatted when things were slow. Two tours in Afghanistan haunted him in ways he couldn't fully express. His spirit was broken. He told me of a friend's mortal wound in Afghanistan. "His blood was dark," he said. "That's how I knew he probably wouldn't make it."

Danny worked hard and got along well with other restaurant team members. When I started building my most recent house on Wellsford Road, I invited him to join the crew. He had no trade, but I valued his work ethic. He dug trenches, hauled trash, drove tractors, moved boulders, and planted trees—anything that needed doing. He did that for three years. It gave him confidence. Then he went out and got a job as a Caltrans conductor and studied to be a train engineer. It could have easily turned out differently. Our country too often grinds up people like Danny and abandons them. They need a safe harbor to find their emotional and financial footing and become high-functioning members of society.

Having a well-functioning team gave me the freedom to interact with customers. I made a habit of walking around and letting people know how much I appreciated them—a practice called *table touching*. I would chat with newlyweds and quietly tell the server to give them a champagne toast and a free dessert. It was utterly unexpected, a memory moment. That interaction gave them a feeling of respect and self-worth. It made the Redwood Café different.

Sometimes, a new restaurant is packed from day one. That never happened with Redwood. We didn't have many customers, even though I put a lot of energy into making it aesthetically appealing the way I thought it should be. It was a slow, depressing grind. I just kept inching forward. Then, after two and a half years, it took off like a freight train. It became unstoppable. It was busy—even on Monday, Tuesday, and Wednesday nights, when most people don't expect a fine-casual restaurant to be full. Those are usually weekend spots, but we created something unique.

Building a fine-casual restaurant was one of the most fulfilling experiences of my business career. It was as if every lesson from my previous ventures had come together, forming something that didn't just work but truly thrived. At the Redwood Café, I had the chance to experiment, innovate, and, occasionally, curse the universe for inventing Yelp. Along the way, I picked up insights that laid the groundwork for other business ideas quietly forming in the back of my mind and opportunities that would pop out of nowhere. I'll get to those in the next chapters, but for now, here are some hard-won lessons that belong in a frame above the desk of every restaurant owner:

**Differentiation is key.** Good food isn't good enough. You need a unique vibe to stand out in the crowded restaurant marketplace. No matter how good your chef is, a generic experience leads to a slow death.

**Every customer has a vote on your future.** Restaurant patrons always judge. They'll tell everyone who'll listen about the experience. If something's off, you're better off hearing it firsthand, so you can fix the issue. Otherwise, you'll find out only when people stop coming.

**You're in a constant contest.** Every meal is silently compared to the best food and service customers have had anywhere. Last week's splurge at a fine-dining spot becomes today's benchmark.

**People's tastes change.** Customer preferences have the shelf life of a ripe avocado. What's popular today could be a snooze tomorrow. You've got to keep up with trends. Adaptation isn't optional; it's survival.

**Servers are your sales force.** Good waiters aren't just order-takers; they're experience-shapers. Whether they're suggesting a second glass of wine or tempting diners with dessert, they play a huge role in guest satisfaction and your bottom line. Servers who can enhance the dining experience are as valuable as any high-profile menu item.

**Every detail counts.** Ambiance, speed, decor—each factor feeds into the guest's impression. Seating comfort, table aesthetics, and layout impact every visit. And owning the space gives you the power to improve it. There's only so much an owner can do to upgrade a rented storefront, and it will show.

**Every moment is a moment of truth.** Quality, taste, presentation, and service all give you the opportunity to create positive or negative memory moments. Neither will be forgotten.

**Margins matter.** Knowing what brings the biggest margins is key to profitability. A bowl of risotto might net ten times more than a steak, even if both sell well.

**Little costs can kill you.** Food spoils fast. Inventory management can be the difference between making a profit or taking a hit.

In the summer of 2020, I got a phone call from the owner of a chain of pizza parlors around Oakdale, a small city about fifteen miles northwest of Modesto. He and his wife occasionally dined at the Redwood Café.

"I have an idea you might be interested in," he said. He admired how I had transformed Vintage Gardens into one of the Central Valley's most popular establishments and wondered if I might consider doing the same thing there. His wife ran a banquet business in a one-hundred-year-old downtown building that had once housed a Dodge dealership and, later, a small brewery. He thought it would be a perfect launch pad for a second Redwood Café.

I demurred. No one knew how or whether the restaurant business would rebound. More importantly, I had other things on my mind. But he and his wife persisted with flattery and financial incentives. They would contribute half a million dollars to renovate the interior according to my design, I would kick in $300,000, and we would split any cost above that. We would co-own the restaurant, which my team would manage day-to-day. I reluctantly agreed—a decision I soon came to regret.

Looking back, I should have been more cautious, given the lingering memory of my previous partnership experience. That relationship left scars: a cautionary tale about unequal commitment and vision that can lead to frustration, misaligned priorities, and a sense of helplessness. Should I have seen red flags here, too, or was this truly a different scenario? Unlike my former partner, these prospective collaborators had established themselves as successful business owners who understood the risks and rewards of the hospitality industry. They were financially committed, eager to create something remarkable, and offered clear incentives. But there were still critical questions I should have asked. Did we genuinely share the same vision? Were we prepared to navigate disagreements over creative and operational decisions? To other entrepreneurs, my advice is this: Scrutinize any partnership as rigorously as you would your business strategy. Seek aligned goals, complementary strengths, and, above all, shared accountability—factors that could have prevented my own regrets, both in the past and now.

My new partners turned out to be what consultants call "seagull managers"—folks who fly in, make a lot of noise, dump on everyone, and fly out. During the two years of construction, they appeared without warning, complained about everything from seating configurations to paint colors, and vanished into the sunset. When the beautiful Redwood Café Oakdale opened in mid-2023, I'd had it with all the drama. I exercised an option to end the arrangement at year's end. The partners rejected an independent business valuation, forcing the issue into arbitration, where it sits as of this writing.

The Redwood Café hosted many quinceañeras, celebrating girls' fifteenth birthdays over the years. Tequila-drinking crowds would spill into the parking lot of the Mormon meeting house next door. Given Mormons' antipathy to alcohol, I was not surprised when church leaders suggested selling me an acre of church land to expand our parking lot. A Salt Lake City official seemed on the verge of a deal but abruptly called it off. After three years of silence, he emailed in 2022: "Please call."

I said, "You guys change your mind?"

"No. We want to buy you."

The church had plans to build a thirty-thousand-square-foot temple on the eighteen-acre site of its aging meetinghouse. I learned that, in a given year, the Mormon Church builds four or five temples in the United States. Its leaders scout the areas to determine whether any nearby properties might pose a problem. If they find an issue, they negotiate to buy it. They did not want to share a block with an establishment that served alcohol. We haggled for three years. I was in a good position but knew there was a limit to what they would pay. When they offered two and a half times the appraised value, I thought, *Either take it or spend the rest of your life regretting it.* When the temple broke ground in October 2023, we closed on a deal that gave me a twenty-month, rent-free lease. I had to vacate by June 2025. I faced a tough decision: Move the Redwood Café, sell it, or shutter it. Whatever happened, a vital piece of Modesto's history and my own would disappear.

I spent about seven or eight months looking for a new place to move the restaurant, but when I ran the numbers, it hit me: Building anything commercial in California was outrageously expensive. If I took the millions the Mormons paid me, then turned around and built something else for millions, what would be the point? The sale had secured my retirement. Why blow it all? In the end, I decided to cannibalize what I could of value from the old restaurant, walk away, and watch the bulldozers trash it. But honestly, that was fine by me—I'd secured my future and moved on.

## Entrepreneurial Life Lessons

- Ambitious entrepreneurs are flexible and alert to opportunities, both within and beyond their familiar territories.

- Skills acquired in one endeavor can provide a fresh perspective in another industry, catapulting them to the front of the pack.

- Relying solely on enthusiasm without a strong grounding in business fundamentals is a recipe for failure.

- Businesses need room to grow organically; push too hard, and you might make strategic mistakes you'll later regret.

# 10

# Rediscovery

## Making True Connections

As we age, life becomes more routine. But the human spirit craves knowledge and new experiences. Wanderlust is in our hearts—at least, it was in mine. I vowed to continue traveling and seeing the world as long as I could wheel a suitcase.

Being of Italian heritage, I longed to see more of Mediterranean Europe and immerse myself in its history, culture, and cuisine. I fantasized about a summer place where I would hang out for three or four months; explore the Dolomites, Piedmont, and Sicily; and introduce my grandchildren to the treasures of Florence and Rome. However, I'd traveled enough to know I would quickly tire of walking up and down streets looking at shop windows and hanging out in museums. I wanted deeper and richer experiences.

Unfortunately, the COVID-19 pandemic shelved such plans for the near future. Italy and other European countries had all but closed their borders to American travelers. To satisfy my cravings, I idly scanned online real estate listings to see what opportunities desperate property owners might offer a cash-ready and patient buyer. An Australian travel company's for-sale ad caught my eye. It conducted aficionado wine tours through Italy, France, Spain, Australia, and New Zealand. The ad didn't say why the owner was selling, but given the widespread lockdowns, it wasn't hard to guess. Out of curiosity, I messaged: "Please tell me more."

My interest was driven by more than a personal urge to hit the road. The COVID-19 crisis had laid bare unsettling truths about society's trajectory. Standing six feet apart, with masks hiding our expressions, suspecting strangers of being walking viral loads, felt like a grim metaphor for the way people were drifting apart in modern life. This isolation hadn't started with the pandemic; it had been creeping in for years as people scattered away from family and community, often in pursuit of jobs, sunshine, or, apparently, the perfect avocado toast. Social media filled the gap by offering instant communication, yes—but also a lot of superficial connections. It was no wonder loneliness had become a tragic epidemic, gnawing at the social fabric with the kind of grim determination that cancer reserves for the human body.

Businesses shared some of the blame—and had become its victims too. In the mad rush for efficiency, many companies had replaced genuine exchanges with digital quick fixes, forgetting that relation-ships were the glue and lubricant that made capitalism work. True connection couldn't be replaced by algorithms or a canned "Thanks for your feedback" message; it was the trust and rapport built through shared experiences that created loyalty and collaboration.

I'd seen firsthand how travel, done right, could be a partial anti-dote to this loneliness. Not the "fifteen countries in seven days" kind of travel that packs you in with hordes of strangers, but experiences that build genuine connections—sharing a meal with locals, forming friendships with fellow travelers, or simply taking the time to absorb a place and its people. In those moments, travel becomes more than an escape; it becomes a way to reconnect with what matters most, a powerful reminder that relationships are at the very core of existence. The more I thought about it, the more I realized the travel business was worth looking into.

Peter Scudamore-Smith answered my email. He said he was well known in the wine industry, one of 416 connoisseurs around the globe awarded the coveted Master of Wine designation by the United Kingdom's Institute of Masters of Wine. His Brisbane consultancy, Uncorked and Cultivated, advised vintners on growing, manufacturing, and marketing. He had developed a side business leading small groups of wine enthusiasts through historic wine regions. That was the part he was looking to sell.

I hadn't considered getting into the travel business, and my knowledge of wine was, to put it mildly, limited, but the more I thought about it, the better it sounded. Once COVID-19 faded, I could offer small group tours to my Redwood Café customers, or maybe lead them myself. What could be more fitting or fun for a seventy-year-old hankering for new travel experiences? Peter's relationships with wineries, hoteliers, and restaurant owners, developed over a quarter of a century, made it a semi-turnkey operation. We negotiated a price of $95,000. I rechristened the little company Redwood Café Tours.

Peter agreed to stay on as an advisor, coach, and tour guide. He would teach me his secret sauce and personally introduce me around. We set out on a grand introductory tour with our wives in the spring of 2022, as Europe slowly awakened from its COVID-19 slumber. I wanted to try on my new business for size, look for ways to improve it, and gain on-the-ground insight into how the tour industry worked. Starting in Portugal, we traveled for weeks, meeting estate owners, winemakers, castle owners, and hotel managers. In France, we explored Épernay, the Champagne region's capital. Located about eighty miles northeast of Paris on the Left Bank of the Marne River, it was home to esteemed Champagne houses like Moët & Chandon, Perrier-Jouët, and Pol Roger. Magnificent mansions lined the famous Avenue de Champagne. Millions of bottles bode their time in subterranean vaults carved into chalky soil. In northern Italy, we met winery owners in Piemonte and then headed to Tuscany and Sicily for more meetings with winery owners, hoteliers, and restaurateurs.

On the flight back to California, I thought like a business owner. Not being a hardcore wine aficionado, I understood how spouses and other tagalongs might tire of long treks through vineyards and discussions of soil acidity and the impact of climate change. How could I broaden the appeal of these tours, add variety, and spice things up without undermining the tours' appeal to serious wine lovers? Should I incorporate activities such as hiking, cycling, or horseback riding through the vineyards? Offer wellness activities like yoga sessions and spa treatments? Add visits to cultural sites, historical landmarks, and other local attractions? My head spun with possibilities.

Lynna and I scheduled another exploratory trip a few months later to test some ideas. We traveled with Peter, his wife, Denise, and members of my restaurant team through France, Spain, and Italy in an upgraded Mercedes van and stayed in nicer hotels. I arranged for the same driver to remain with us throughout our journey, so he would become familiar with our preferences, routines, and personalities, and everyone would get to know him. I asked that he meet us curbside every morning to get things off to a prompt and stress-free start and be open to unscheduled stops and occasional detours to increase the feeling of freedom and adventure. That enabled us to discover quaint, family-owned wineries, charming roadside cafés, and little Tuscan farmstands that were not on the itinerary. As I knew from running a restaurant, unexpected delights transform routine experiences into precious memories.

In Florence, the van delivered us to Ora d'Aria, a Michelin-starred restaurant on a quiet street behind the Uffizi Gallery. The manager, Federico, greeted Peter with open arms and a big smile. The ambiance was modern and elegant, and its minimalist design contrasted with Florence's rich historical backdrop. The open kitchen gave us an unobstructed view of the vaunted culinary team at work.

Marco Stabile had a reputation as one of Florence's most innovative chefs. Before we opened our menus, Federico returned. Marco wanted to introduce his latest creation personally. The famous chef appeared. A dashing figure—think Marcello Mastroianni at his peak. In heavily accented English, he described what he had in mind: three versions of Tuscan cuisine—past, present, and future. The first would be traditional farmhouse cooking, the second a contemporary version, the third a reinvention using innovative tech. He smiled. "*Buon appetito!*" It was the crowning moment of our adventure.

Surrounded by acquaintances old and new, buoyed by laughter and camaraderie, I couldn't help reflecting on how our journey differed from most others. Technology, budget airlines, giant cruise ships, and package deals made exploring the world much easier and cheaper than when I boarded my first Pan Am flight two generations earlier. But something important got lost along the way. Modern tourists hustled between overcrowded destinations, disconnected from the essence of their surroundings. Homogenized experiences lacked spontaneity and depth. Travelers missed out on off-the-beaten-path discoveries that made journeys memorable. Vibrant communities had become selfie backdrops, leaving travelers and locals shortchanged. Cultural immersion lost out to speed and convenience. I decided that my mission would be to offer an alternative—a return to travel as it should be.

I was convinced that small-group travel, done right, could counteract the pervasive ennui of modern life. Shared adventures build friendships. Hitting the road or hopping on a Lufthansa flight pushes people out of their comfort zones. Unfamiliar landscapes, cuisines, and cultures provide a sense of purpose and create opportunities for meaningful human connections. Chatting with fellow travelers on long train rides, sharing meals with locals at a bustling café, or exchanging smiles with strangers on crowded streets reminds people that they are threads in an intricate tapestry.

Peter, Lynna, and I sat on the terrace of the boutique Hotel Villa Schuler in Taormina, a picturesque Sicilian town famous for quaint streets and views overlooking the Ionian Sea and Mount Etna, Europe's highest and most active volcano. Taormina exuded history, with roots tracing back to the fourth-century BC Greeks. Its landscapes have made it a favorite destination for celebrities and high-profile travelers alike, and it even served as the luxurious backdrop for season two of HBO's hit show *The White Lotus*. From our vantage point, we could see the resort where it was filmed down below.

"I want you to meet Gerhart Schuler, the owner of this hotel," Peter said. "And Mr. Schuler wants to know you." Soon, Gerhart and his wife, Christine, joined us for cocktails. Gerhart told us how his German artist grandfather had come to Sicily in the late nineteenth century, becoming known for his photographs of Sicilian life. He made a fortune selling antique furniture to touring Victorians and became a successful hotelier. The Italian government confiscated the hotel during World War I. The family repurchased it after the war but lost it again in World War II. When it went to auction after the war, no one bid against the family. Gerhart said he would eventually pass control to his son, Andrea, a former New York ballet dancer.

Listening to Gerhart recount his story, I realized how much I enjoyed connecting with someone with deep roots in the area. I was no longer just Bob in room 14—I was a flesh-and-blood individual. It transformed a destination into an unforgettable experience. Now I had the opportunity to share these kinds of experiences. The travel business as I envisioned it would invite people into my world, diving deep into cultures, not just skimming the surface. I wanted to give people experiences they would have no way of creating independently.

As I approached the age of seventy, you'd think I'd be content with slippers and stock portfolios. But there I was, still getting a rush from brainstorming a new business idea, as if it was the first time I'd waded into these waters. Of course, a start-up is always a leap into the unknown. There's no Google Maps for this journey—just a lot of questions, few answers, and maybe a flashlight with half-dead batteries. You pick up what you can, trust your instincts, and just try to adapt before things go sideways.

Registering my new venture as Redwood Café Tours, I got a California travel license. Then I approached the travel industry like an archaeologist, with a shovel, a brush, and a very vague treasure map. How would this thing work exactly? What's the deal with pricing, market segmentation, and tour arrangements? Thanks to past successes, capital wasn't the concern. But I knew I'd need a solid copilot with the right skills to help get things off the ground.

That's where Lino Mansoni, my son-in-law, came in. Lino, Katrina's husband, was well traveled, multilingual, and sharp as a tack, with a background that included tech stints in Dublin and San Francisco. Raised in Paris, his father had led Zaire through a civil war before turning a Parisian taxicab association into something of a mini empire. Growing up with one foot in each of these worlds, Lino brought the kind of cultural radar I knew would be critical to running international tours. His connections would help us line up the right partnerships, and his insights would keep us from launching a tour of "local" experiences that just ended up as Instagram backdrops.

Lino and I both agreed that the future was in luxury, small-group travel. People wanted immersive, customized experiences—the opposite of mass-market tours—and they were willing to pay for it. They were done being shuttled around in massive buses with stopovers at tourist-trap shops. They wanted comfort, exclusivity, and a taste of authenticity—without the endless hours of scrolling through Tripadvisor to find it. And let's be clear: They weren't looking for bargains; they were looking for well-curated journeys where someone else had done the legwork.

Peter's wine tour business was a good foundation, but it lacked that spark of discovery. When Lynna and I did a European winery tour with him, the first few stops were amazing. But after three winery visits a day, every day, we'd had enough. We were thirsty for something different—a balance of structure and serendipity. In Italy, I had a vision for what our tours would be. Imagine spotting a beautiful hillside village on the way to lunch and actually being able to go check it out rather than hearing "Sorry, lunch reservations."

I knew then that my tour business would be more hands-on than I'd first imagined. And I didn't mind that one bit. I wanted to explore the world with people who, like me, preferred quality over convenience and personal experience over canned itineraries. It gave me the perfect combination of challenge and travel—plus, let's face it, I was the ideal customer.

To succeed in the travel business, I needed to speak with authority. There was no better way to get my finger on the travel market's pulse than attending ITB Berlin, the industry's leading trade show. In late winter 2023, I flew to Germany's capital with Lino and three people who normally helped me on various business and personal projects. They were my team for the week. How could I plan small-group travel without a group? We checked into a modern little accommodation called the B&B Hotel Berlin-Charlottenburg. Expedia called it "budget friendly," and it was, but not in a negative way; there were no uniformed bellhops, and breakfast was self-serve muesli, yogurt, and coffee. I was still wondering how fancy a hotel our intended clients might expect. A five-star place might be too far removed from the local culture, but I was thinking too far ahead.

ITB took over the massive Messe Berlin exhibition center, serving as the central hub for information and opportunities—a place to meet people and explore options. Travel agencies, tour operators, booking systems, airlines, hotels, and representatives from 180 countries filled the venue's twenty-six interconnected halls. They showcased their products, services, and destinations, hoping to boost their visibility, attract tourists, develop contacts, and negotiate deals with industry partners.

We wandered among large displays promoting Iran and Seychelles, as well as through multimedia extravaganzas featuring India and Saudi Arabia. I moved from exhibit to exhibit, assessing each one. This occurred almost wordlessly, in minutes if not seconds. It resembled a subliminal experience; I made eye contact with someone, and that connection either led to further interaction or just moving on.

I also had a pocket full of business cards and a collection of ribboned medals engraved with the phrase "Bob's Favorite" to award promising prospects. The latter was a clever old-school salesman's trick, a playful way to establish rapport and set myself apart from the sea of suits. It created small but memorable interactions, adding levity and recognition people appreciated. When I handed someone a medal, it felt like an award—a mini validation that subtly built goodwill and left a lasting impression. It served as a perfect icebreaker and a fun way to start a conversation.

A young man at the little Bulgarian booth nodded brightly as I floated the idea of a ten-person food-and-wine-centric tour of the country in a luxury transit van. Whom, I asked, might I work with there to make it happen? He fingered my card and promised to email suggestions. A sarong-clad young woman in the Borneo booth touted rafting expeditions down the Kiulu River. An older gentleman in a black-and-white kalpak urged me to trek the Kyrgyz Republic's Tian Shan Mountains. Hour after hour, my little entourage walked the floor, telling Redwood Café Tours' story. My goal was not to sign contracts but to get a feel for the travel business, gather ideas, and spark relationships. In that, I succeeded. I left the convention hall that evening with a notebook full of names, sore feet, and a big appetite.

When visiting a new city, I typically ask a cab company to send me a born-and-bred native driver who knows out-of-the-way dives where locals gather. Taxi Berlin sent me Hans, a fifty-ish-year-old man who spoke broken English. I asked him to take us to the city's best schnitzel restaurant. Twenty minutes later, he pulled in front of a brightly lit, one-story building in the Mitte district bearing a small plaque that said *Schnitzelei* in antique German letters. I invited Hans to join our crew for dinner, and he eagerly accepted. Rough-hewn tables lined bright, noisy dining rooms. Young waiters hustled about carrying mugs and glasses on shoulder trays. It was just what I had hoped for. As we spilled, laughing, into the winter darkness two hours later, the owner stood by the door. "*Sie bald wieder!*" he said. *Come back soon!* And that we did—on every evening of our four-day Berlin stay. By night three, our table was set, our beers were open, and our plates of bratwurst were coming out of the kitchen by the time we got our coats off. We felt like regulars in the old TV show *Cheers*.

My nerves were tingling. It was the kind of experience that Redwood Café Tours would be about. It was an ambitious goal— one that might take years to fully realize. It would require forming relationships with hundreds of transportation providers, hotel and restaurant owners, shop owners, and members of country tourism offices.

Chance plays an unheralded role in business success. Although innovation and strategy are essential, it helps to be in the right place at the right time. The following day, at ITB, I got lucky. Stopping by the Sicilian booth, I introduced myself to an unassuming gentleman browsing his phone. He explained that he was a businessman there to promote the island. As I eventually discovered, Giuseppe Giorgianni was being too modest. He was a pioneering entrepreneur and international business leader who traveled the globe helping companies implement transformative technologies. He owned several companies, one of which introduced an award-winning wearable that let physicians check the health of individual patients in remote third-world areas. One of his other ventures was the central opera house in Taormina.

Giuseppe introduced me to his friend, Francesco Fratantonio, a jovial man who, I discovered, owned seven Sicilian luxury hotels. I suggested they join our group for dinner that night; I would look for a restaurant. Francesco smiled and raised his index finger. "*Un momento,"* he said. He pressed a few digits on his phone, said a few words in Italian, and turned back to us. He said the Italian embassy would reserve a banquet table for us at one of Berlin's top Italian restaurants. We spent that evening making cheerful conversation and rousing toasts. "You must come to see me soon," Francesco said, giving me a bear hug as we parted.

A few months later, he welcomed Lynna and me to Sicily like old friends and led us on a tour of Sicily's quaint villages, including the town of Catania, an ancient Greek settlement all but destroyed by earthquakes in 1169 and 1693. Francesco had restored two buildings into hotels. In a seventeenth-century church, he pointed to a rope leading to the belfry. Since my surname was the Italian word for *bell,* he said, it was only proper to ring it. He grinned as I broke the little town's silence.

In Taormina, Giuseppe invited us to dine with him and his wife, the noted soprano Silvia Di Falco. She had just flown in from performances in Tel Aviv, Dubai, and London. We relaxed on the opera house deck over the Ionian. Silvia told me about forthcoming gigs in New York and Los Angeles. The latter, I said, would coincide with my planned seventieth birthday party. Would she be my guest? Of course! That was how 180 guests came to enjoy Sicilian food, wine, and a never-to-forget performance by a world-class soprano. In the future, when I took customers of Redwood Café Tours to Sicily, we'd attend the Taormina opera and dine with Giuseppe, Silvia, and the performers afterward. It would be a rare experience that my travel guests would always remember.

My decision to get into the small-group tour business could not have come at a better time. In the pandemic's wake, travelers were wary of cramming onto a floating resort with five thousand unknown people or massing shoulder to shoulder at popular destinations. After hibernating for a year or more, they craved human interaction and more intimate experiences. I wasn't alone in recognizing the opportunity. Boutique travel agencies, educational institutions, and adventure groups responded by partnering with on-the-ground tour and transportation providers worldwide.

Small-group tours offered broad cultural experiences and special-interest adventures catering to niche passions like wine, food, photography, or rock climbing. Although regional wine tours would remain our bread and butter for now, Lino and I also eyed single-country cultural excursions to Italy, Japan, and Australia.

Customized, activity-oriented tours were potentially more profitable, but more of a challenge to conceptualize, market, and conduct. I had no idea which, of a thousand narrow markets, most of which I had never heard of, would support two- and three-week excursions costing anywhere from $5,000 to $25,000. How could we credibly connect with them, come up with compelling tour themes, and persuade them to travel with us? Surveying the touring and media landscapes, I concluded that there was only one plausible answer: social media. Every conceivable interest had one or more Facebook, Instagram, YouTube, or TikTok channels. Content creators, or "influencers," attracted huge, narrowly focused audiences. Could we collaborate with them to develop ideas and sell the trips?

As a test, my niece Marie Schermeister, a recent graduate of the University of California, Davis, emailed eighty cold queries to random influencers. A young woman with half a million TikTok and twice that many Instagram followers proposed a fashion trip to Europe. An agent for the professional football player and prolific online video game player Marquise "Hollywood" Brown suggested traveling with fans to Tokyo, where they would immerse themselves in the world's most vibrant gaming community. Would such ideas fly? Who knew? As I reminded my team, opportunities pop up in unexpected places. We would have to figure things out as we went along.

Building a travel business involves a lot of behind-the-scenes mechanics. Once a tour was conceptualized and sold, someone had to manage the logistics. Lino and Marie would do the heavy lifting. Every detail had to run like clockwork to keep the experience smooth and stress-free, from timely airport pickups to restaurant reservations. Each component—drivers, hotels, activities, and meals—had to mesh seamlessly so travelers would not feel rushed or distracted by logistics. In this business, even minor hiccups would detract from the experience. The value wasn't just the destination but how effortlessly the journey unfolded. That was where our on-the-ground affiliates, known as "destination tour operators," or simply "destination operators," came in. Local knowledge was needed to plan detailed itineraries, coordinate logistics, and identify unique experiences.

Selecting reliable operators wasn't always straightforward. We met plenty at ITB, but I needed firsthand experience before trusting them with clients. I was also on the lookout for individual tour guides—people with that magic touch—like Davide, whom I met at ITB's Italian booth. He was young, managed a couple of hotels in Sicily, and had an easy charm. I gave him a test run in Sicily a few months later, where he was such a hit that I asked him to lead six Redwood clients through Sardinia on a $94,000 private tour. Guests came back raving about him. It could've gone the other way; he might have been unreliable, leaving us with a train wreck of a trip. But he nailed it.

Through personal trial and error, I also figured out the ideal ground transport: an eight-person van for every five guests. Anything more than that, and it felt like economy class—too cramped, too close. With the right van setup, it was a bit like flying business class: just enough room to stretch out and not feel like you're stuck shoulder to shoulder for hours.

By the end of 2024, Redwood Café Tours was a work in progress—a venture packed with potential but not yet at the point of steady profit. But I had the patience and stubbornness to see it through. One hard-won lesson in business is that ventures rarely move at the pace you'd like; they run on their own time. Three years after buying the company from Peter, I was still piecing together my vision. Where did I really want to take this? And more importantly, how would I get there? Trying to answer both questions at once was, to put it mildly, a challenge. At times, I wondered if I was chasing a fool's errand. But I knew from experience that this was the usual path for any worthwhile business.

## Entrepreneurial Life Lessons

- Loneliness has become a tragic epidemic, gnawing at the social fabric with grim determination.

- Unfamiliar landscapes, cuisines, and cultures provide a sense of purpose and create opportunities for meaningful human connections.

- Although innovation and strategy are essential, it helps to be in the right place at the right time.

- Ventures rarely move at the pace you'd like; they run on their own time.

# 11

# YouTube

## Learning New Tricks

They say there's no zealot like a convert. I never imagined that, in my latter years, I'd dive headfirst into social media. But on the eve of my seventieth birthday, I launched *GetBack2Work!*, a YouTube channel for people to follow along as I built new restaurants, flew over the Central Valley, and explored the world. Why not? I had decades of experience to share, with plenty of new adventures ahead. Still, it was a reluctant leap. For years, I'd held strong opinions about social media—mainly that it was making people miserable, convincing them their lives fell short of others' glossy, filtered versions. But then I realized there was another side: Technology could also connect people, share experiences, and create bonds. I took the plunge and didn't look back.

The learning curve was steep, but every video taught me something—from lighting techniques to storytelling. Authenticity was key. I quickly assembled a team—novices mostly, in keeping with my belief that enthusiasm, a fresh eye, and the desire to learn often trump experience. Sure, we made rookie mistakes, but it was fun.

Marky "Mark" Phillips, an ex-Marine, became our expert on drone and video shots. Garrett Vick, a writer-turned-cinematographer, kept us laughing with puns and creative angles on everything. Mark's sister, April Phillips, and Javier Ruiz, a former manager at Redwood Café, took on editing, turning our footage into nearly professional-grade videos.

We made it up as we went, piecing together an ad hoc system that somehow worked. April and Javier sent rough cuts to a small Lithuanian company for final polishing, then layered in narration and music. Bringing in a pro would've been more efficient, but it felt more rewarding to puzzle it out ourselves.

At first, I saw the YouTube channel as a marketing tool for the travel business. But once I got rolling, I couldn't resist posting videos on my other ventures—helicopter flights, restaurant tours, even explorations in the Australian outback. The result was a bit scattershot—not exactly a marketing powerhouse for any single business.

Then someone pointed out something I'd overlooked: I was the common thread. In every video, whether flying high, chatting with patrons, or discussing the carvings on an ancient Sevillian church door, I was the constant. It hit me that the channel didn't need to promote any one venture—it could be about sharing my entrepreneurial journey, making "Bob Campana" the brand itself.

If you've ever watched *Magnum, P.I.*, with Tom Selleck, you might remember how every episode ends with the creator Stephen J. Cannell's signature flashing across the screen. I loved that move. So I found a company on TikTok to create a similar tag for my videos. Now, every clip ends with my own mark—my name, my brand. Hollywood, here I come!

Could I actually make money with this YouTube thing? That thought crossed my mind more than once. But here's the reality: Almost nobody succeeds. Out of eighty-seven million YouTube channels, fewer than sixty thousand are monetized. To even qualify, you need one thousand subscribers and four thousand watch hours in a year.

By the end of 2024, I had about 800 subscribers and 2,900 watch hours. So, I was 200 subscribers and 1,100 watch hours short of monetization. Most of my short videos got around 500 views, but one suddenly shot up to 11,000. Naturally, I wanted to know why. What was different? The topic? The pacing? I found myself dissecting it, second by second, as if I were analyzing a crime scene.

I also studied the YouTube algorithm. They push out a small set of videos to test the waters. If viewers click and stick around, it goes to more people, then more again, expanding its reach. There's a method to it, and I was keen to crack the code—because if you can pull in millions of viewers, YouTube can turn into a fantastic income stream.

Meanwhile, Redwood Café Tours kept evolving. I made a second, more productive, trip to ITB, followed by a scouting mission to Australia and New Zealand with my remarkably patient wife, Lynna, and my intrepid associate Lorna. We started in Brisbane, then headed north to Cairns, discovering a tropical paradise. The Great Barrier Reef was too churned up for snorkeling, so we chatted with the boat captain instead.

In the Northern Territory, near Darwin, we met the thirty-two-year-old owner of Finish River Ranch, a fifty-thousand-acre cattle station she'd inherited from her grandfather. During the rainy season, cattle get stranded on little islands, which made them easy pickings for crocodiles. The ranchers couldn't legally kill the protected crocs, so they hired brave souls to relocate them—no easy task.

At Kakadu National Park, we watched the sunrise over the Yellow Water, a river thick with reptiles, before catching the legendary Ghan railroad to South Australia. In Alice Springs, our bus driver, a retired detective, told us about a family who had lost a child to a croc while out with an inexperienced river guide.

Coober Pedy was unforgettable. Known for opal mines and underground homes, it's a surreal landscape dotted with two million mining shafts and mounds of talcum powder–like dirt. The stuff acts like quicksand if it falls back into the shafts—unaware walkers beware. Half the town lives underground to escape the heat.

In Adelaide, Peter took us through six or seven wineries before we reached Sydney, where we saw the Opera House and watched a sold-out *Harry Potter* screening with live accompaniment from a 220-piece orchestra.

New Zealand was the next adventure, and somewhere along the way, I convinced Lynna and Lorna—or maybe they convinced me—to bungee jump off Auckland's fifty-three-story tower. We hit eighty-five miles an hour on the way down. Then we took a helicopter to Mount Cook and Tasman Glacier and boarded the TSS *Earnslaw* steamship on Lake Wakatipu, and I gave a medal to the helpful engineer, who showed it off to the captain. When the captain looked a little slighted, I pulled another from my bag for him.

Driving around New Zealand's South Island, I pulled our small rental car into a lookout above Queenstown to take in the sheep-dotted fields, church steeples, a stunning lake, and The Remarkables mountain range rising above Lake Wakatipu. A Porsche with the plate number 911 GTS was parked nearby. I recognized it as the top-end model—carbon fiber roof, mirrors, and bucket seats. A man in his fifties with a salt-and-pepper beard leaned against it, phone in hand, while a young woman, who I assumed was his trophy girlfriend, lounged nearby. I approached him with my Osmo Action 3 videocam and asked, "Mind if I take some videos of your car?" He looked up. "No problem."

After a few minutes, he asked, "You wouldn't happen to have any water, would you?" I grabbed a quart from my car and handed it over. He opened the rear engine hatch, unscrewed a cap, and poured the water in. "It's overheating," he said. "I just got it back from the shop and can't figure it out." I gave him a couple more bottles.

He introduced himself as Rod Drury and the woman as Susie. Then he asked, "Are you into cars? Want to see my collection?" Susie eagerly nodded behind him, so I said, "Sure." Rod punched his address into my phone and said, "Follow me." However, two miles down the road, the Porsche's engine blew—smoke poured out of the back—and he pulled over.

Rod calmly made a phone call, and we all got into my rental car. His house was the size of a small palace.

The huge garage held dozens of cars. I spotted a Porsche 918 Spyder, worth over a million dollars, and a Ferrari Dino, a rare model produced in the late '60s and early '70s in honor of Enzo Ferrari's deceased son. There were also a couple of Range Rovers. He tapped on the window of a stealthy black Rolls Royce Silver Shadow and smiled. "I only drive this one at night," he said. I think he was joking.

He took us to another house, under construction, a few miles away. Behind the main structure, a large annex was rising—a future conference room, he said, for highly classified conversations. It would be soundproofed with electromagnetic shielding to block electronic surveillance, so the government could use it for national security meetings. It didn't seem like the right moment to ask why they'd use his house instead of a government facility.

The whole experience felt too strange to be real, like I'd stumbled into a high-stakes thriller. Back at the hotel, I did a little digging on Rod. Not only was he legitimate, but he was one of New Zealand's wealthiest men, the founder of Xero, a cloud-based accounting software giant. As for the government meetings? There was nothing public on that, but then again—would there be? A few days later, Rod emailed me to thank me for the water. He explained that a loose plug had caused oil to leak, which led to the overheating. Porsche was handling the repairs, and everything was fine.

How did a random stop lead to an encounter with one of the world's richest men? Pure happenstance; that's the beauty of peripatetic travel. Why did we develop a bit of a bond? Hard to say, but I have a theory that I call "the bullshit meter." Successful people have a good sense of who's genuine. When people meet me, I think they sense I'm not trying to get anything from them. I'm just someone interesting to talk to. The ultra-wealthy live in a different world, but sometimes they choose to let you in.

After two days of home recovery from the New Zealand adventure, I was off again, this time to Slovakia, where Daniel Von Rechitar, a descendant of the fifteenth-century nobleman Vlad II Dracul, inducted me into the ancient Order of the Dragon. Dracul's son, Vlad III, inspired Bram Stoker's *Dracula*. Recognizing the potential tourist appeal, the Slovakian government urged Daniel to turn Dracul's castle ruin into a five-star hotel. It was a potential tour destination and another great YouTube opportunity.

My seventieth birthday party, on December 28, 2023, was one of the most memorable nights of my life. Lynna and our daughters decided to throw a big celebration for this milestone—quite special for a guy who rarely has birthday parties. In fact, the last big one was for my fiftieth, and even then, I didn't make a habit of it. Usually, it's just me, Lynna, the kids, and the grandkids. But Lynna insisted this was important.

We had around 180 people there, almost more than the room could handle. Lynna reserved the Oakdale restaurant, just before I sold it. It was my final goodbye, a fitting end to an unhappy episode in my life. I donned a bright red blazer and joined the guests to enjoy a remarkable performance by my Sicilian opera singer friend, Silvia Di Falco. "It is a gift for you," she said.

I stood in the back as Silvia asked everyone to raise their glasses. The whole room turned to me, all those faces full of love and warmth, and sang "Happy Birthday." I don't usually get emotional, but that got to me. Seeing all those people there, knowing they showed up for me, really touched me.

I was hard to miss in the packed room. Just a day before, Annie's husband, Andy, a designer and hairdresser in Austin, Texas, called and said, "Bob, you're turning seventy; you need a proper outfit." I hadn't thought about it at all, but he convinced me. I ended up at Joe Rossini's menswear store, and Joe, an old friend, put together a great red coat and outfit. He didn't even charge me—said it was his birthday gift to me. So there I was, in that red coat, unmistakable in the crowd.

Looking around the room, I thought, *This is what a life well-lived looks like.* People don't just show up like that unless there's something real between you. I felt honored, not only by friends and family but also by my employees—people like Marky Mark and Garrett, who came out to celebrate with me. Having so many people willing to spend their Thursday evening with me is something I'll never forget.

My third daughter, Audrey, brought the room to laughter, recounting the thrills and embarrassments of life in the Campana household. At the back of the room, greeting guests, I couldn't hear a lot of what she said, so I asked her to send me a copy. Here it is in full for your enjoyment:

> Our dad used to get asked a lot, "Wow, what's it like being the only man in the house with your wife and four daughters?" And he'd always answer, "It's not so bad; they let me get a male dog . . . but then they made me neuter him." That's the PG version of his response.
>
> Likewise, we have all been asked, "What's it like growing up with Bob as your dad?" more times than we can count. The answer is truly longer than anyone regularly has time to hear, and we usually attribute our well-being to our saint of a mother, but tonight seemed like the perfect time to answer this question and paint a fuller picture.
>
> Growing up with Bob as our dad was a lot of the expected . . . bedtime stories in his armchair, sponsored sports teams called Vintage Gardens Cater Raiders or Vintage Gardens Brunch Bunch, trips to Vintage Pool Company to visit him at the office, birthday parties, and so on.
>
> But the majority of our childhood memories were the UNEXPECTED:
>
> • Being hung from the beams in our living room.
>
> • The famous "New Guinea death drops," which involved being flung upside down and suspended from our ankles after recovering from the whiplash of a sudden drop.

- Uncomfortable "nose sucks" instead of kisses as a form of twisted endearment.

- Newly innovative built-in BBQs in the early '90s catching fire in the backyard.

- Summers spent listening to the Whitney Houston *Bodyguard* soundtrack and Elton John for over ten consecutive years (definitely played at top volume when Dad was exercising on his NordicTrack).

- Abandoning a ski boat in the middle of Don Pedro that had also caught fire, and then forcing high school girls to swim/tow him back to shore.

- The fire department showing up at our graduation party because Dad made a record-sized bonfire for us and our friends to burn our Catholic school uniforms.

- Showing up in Washington, DC, with our eighth-grade class and realizing Dad had brought his own umbrella for the group to follow, fully intending to be the head tour guide (proceeding to give socially insensitive training on how to fake a handicap to get to the front of the line at the Smithsonian).

- Having our dad greet high school peers while wearing white spandex shorts long before yoga pants or spandex were socially acceptable.

- Developing a healthy respect for Dad's perfectly manicured lawns—Caroline was once told she couldn't mow the lawns because she didn't know proper lawn patterns. No one understands the repercussions of tire marks veering off his narrow driveway into his meticulously irrigated, seed-grown, overly nurtured lawn.

- Having a thirty-watt LED bullet floodlight as a nightlight out your window because Dad had the highest residential flagpole in the area, proudly displaying an American flag, as he is the biggest patriot we know.

- Taking flight lessons to hover a helicopter before having a driver's license.

- Coming home from the St. Stanislaus fall festival with a Watusi bull after Dad heckled donors about bringing a cow worth bidding on at the auction.

- Realizing after fourteen years that we'd been pronouncing our sister Annie's name wrong when landing in Italy and Dad's long-lost Italian accent emerged, introducing her as "ONnie."

- Caroline spending an entire vacation in an unrelenting dead-leg battle with Dad, only to be taken down by the ultimate final hit behind the knees, dropping her mid-step at the front of the TSA line in a North Carolina airport (no surprise, Dad was ushered aside for additional screening).

- Having a bag of birdseed thrown at your feet in the middle of St. Mark's Square in Venice and watching your dad walk away smugly in his tourist fanny pack as a sea of pigeons descended.

- Inviting priests over for family dinner and doing a wardrobe change to serve dessert in tiger-print pants.

- Always guaranteed he would deliver the most politically incorrect joke imaginable at high volume to a mixed group . . . then laugh the hardest at his own punchline.

But now that we have all survived the unexpected of being raised by Bob, and have been properly treated by optometrists after decades of viewing blue LED lights incorporated into pool, landscape, and now interior designs . . . we can truly appreciate all the lessons in life he has taught us along the way. We can all attribute our wit and strong senses of humor to our dad. He is one of the hardest-working individuals we know and provided us with a life full of opportunities. No matter what idea or aspirations we had, he was the first to encourage us and ask how he could help us achieve our goals.

Anyone who knows our dad knows he has a heart of gold, is the biggest animal lover, always sees the best in people, is genuine, honest, and always has the most sincere intentions. He thrives as a grandpa, spending an unhealthy amount of time scheming elaborate pranks to play on the kids, showering them with love, and adopting their individual interests as his own. He is a self-educated man who could easily be a professor of business, political science, economics, or world and US history based on his constant reading, quest for knowledge, and world travel. He valued our education and instilled in each of us his strong entrepreneurial spirit. Together with our mom, they have shown us the perfect example of a successful, loving marriage full of compromise (mostly on Lynna's part) for the past forty-two years, something we each aspire to.

It's almost a guarantee that he will know someone everywhere we go, and he will always be the life of the party in any room. We are thrilled to have all his family and friends in this room tonight to celebrate him for his seventieth birthday. So let's raise our glasses to our dad, Bobbi, Uncle Bob, Papa Bob, Helicopter Bob, Rancher Bob, Vintage Pools Bob, Talk Radio Taking Care of Business Bob, Helicopter Plumber Bob, Contractor Bob, Tour Guide Bob, Vintage Gardens, and Redwood Café Bob . . . or any variation of Bob you've grown to know and love over the years. Cheers to Bob!

Watching that poised young woman regale my dearest friends touched me beyond words and made me proud.

Wrestling with the Oakdale seagulls had convinced me that I was done building restaurants. The restaurant game was for a younger, more energetic soul. I figured I'd focus on the tour business. But then Ed Maring—the eighty-five-year-old grandfather of Audrey's husband, Zachary Maring—came to me with a pitch: He wanted to turn a historic building he owned in the small town of Patterson into an upscale dining spot. Hard to say no to family, especially when Ed was looking at this as his legacy. A successful farmer, Ed wanted to give something back to the community his family had been part of for generations. "The town needs a gathering place, like in the old days," he said. And he was right. Patterson needed a social hub, and his building—the Old Water Office—needed preservation.

Still, I hesitated, questioning if I had it in me to tackle another major project. Gutting the building, wrestling with the city's building, public works, and health departments, not to mention designing a unique ambiance, developing a menu, and assembling a team—it was a mountain of work. But Ed was ready to put up the $2.4 million construction cost, planning to own the restaurant and make just enough to cover his investment. He wasn't in it to get rich, just to avoid saddling his family with losses. I agreed to design and manage the project at no charge, and we'd split any future profits.

Once committed, I went full speed ahead—there wasn't any other way I knew. This project offered me a chance to create something lasting for the town, something that might even outlast me. The technical work was daunting. We hired an architect for structural plans, an engineer for building codes and earthquake reinforcement, and brought on specialists for electrical and HVAC specs. Just getting the permits required a five-inch-thick roll of plans and cost more than $100,000.

My focus was on the interior design. The architect, buttering me up, had said, "Look, Bob, I can't do what you do." I'd developed a love for designing spaces over the years, especially from my work landscaping pools. For this project, I chose an authentic mission style inspired by Spanish architecture. I even traveled to Spain for ideas on tile work, window coverings, and the rest. My design featured wire-cut brick walls, vintage glass windows, ceiling beams crafted from old Southern Pacific railroad ties, and an iron stairway winding up to the second-floor dining room. Every element was custom—no

Home Depot shortcuts here. I even enlisted two craftsmen to make chandeliers and fixtures in the workshop behind my house.

Typically, a project like this would need a big team, but I took on a lot of it myself—not out of a Superman complex, but because every detail mattered. Managing it all was a constant juggling act, with the city tossing in hurdles left and right. One major headache came courtesy of an ancient underground water pipe. The city had granted us a public alley for outdoor dining, but it was lined with century-old pipes. We agreed to replace all the pipes in our area, only for the city to demand we upgrade to an eight-inch pipe with extra valves. That alone set us back $70,000. I called in the city's public works and building inspectors, laid out the situation, and reminded them that they were budgeted to replace these pipes in 2025 anyway. So why was this on us? I submitted a bill for reimbursement—it was an $80,000 job that, by all rights, shouldn't have come out of our budget. The town grudgingly paid it.

The Old Water Office, a Redwood Café Group Restaurant, was set to open in January 2025, effectively replacing the Modesto location. My experienced team—Lorna, Gerry, and my bar manager, Chris Hull—would run it. With the community's support and Ed's standing in town, I thought it might just be the crowning achievement of my career.

## Entrepreneurial Life Lessons

- Although technology contributes to loneliness, it can also connect people, share experiences, and create bonds.

- In a new venture, enthusiasm, a fresh eye, and the desire to learn often trump experience.

- Successful people have a good sense of who's genuine and who's not.

# 12

# River Islands

## Creating a Legacy

What was I to make of that creative energy, that mysterious life spice that drove me on even after I'd scaled so many mountains and checked off all unmet financial needs? I might as well have asked Martin Scorsese and Clint Eastwood what kept them cranking out movies in their eighties and nineties—not that I was in their league. I still had the same entrepreneurial hunger I'd felt on Bayshore Parkway at age twenty-one and the energy to go with it. Some credited the cans of Red Bull I kept around like holy relics. But I knew it was more than that; I felt it in the whir of a helicopter, the thrill of standing on a ledge with a bungee cord, or the unmistakable ring of opportunity.

That ring came one bright April morning, on a day smelling of damp earth and almond blossoms, with finches serenading in the distance. In reality, it was my iPhone, dinging to inform me of a call from my 209 area code—a reassuring sign that it probably wasn't another spam pitch for an expiring car warranty.

"Mr. Campana?"

The caller introduced herself as the assistant to the CEO of The Campay Group, a company that owned River Islands, a sprawling development in Lathrop, twenty miles north of Modesto. She said her boss, Susan Dell'Osso, a fan of the Redwood Café, wanted to talk about a potential business relationship. I didn't know much about River Islands beyond its fame as one of Northern California's largest projects. It was a buzzing new community of upscale homes that generated environmental controversy and breathless praise in the press. Susan got straight to the point: While River Islands had lakeside beauty, prospective buyers wanted more than nice views. They wanted a sense of community, with shops, gathering places, and a splash of urban flair to keep things lively. And one of those essentials? A first-class restaurant.

We met at the Patterson construction site. I figured she'd appreciate seeing how much work went into creating a restaurant—sweat, sawdust, and the occasional bureaucratic headache. She was polished, with an easygoing confidence. Right away, I sensed a positive aura, a life energy. Most people in the know would fawn over Susan Dell'Osso, aware of her financial power. I'd learned long ago that approaching people like that got relationships off to a bad start. I wanted to signal we were on the same level, so I politely said, "Look, I'm at a stage where I won't do anything I don't want to do. I'm interviewing you to see if I might want to work with you, and maybe you're doing the same." I could tell she respected that.

As we walked the construction site, she seemed impressed. She explained that River Islands had been searching for something unique. They had a chain restaurant, but it wasn't special enough. They needed something distinctive, and thought the Redwood

Café could be the missing piece. I mentioned my plan to close the Modesto location by spring of 2025. "Maybe you could just move it," she said casually.

Her directness threw me off. I suspected this was where things were heading, but hearing it as an actual proposal made it real. It rattled me—it meant rethinking what I thought my seventies would look like. She must have seen my "deer in the headlights" look. "Why don't you sit down with Allan Chapman?" she suggested.

Allan was the head of Cambay's parent company, Somerston Holdings, a private investment firm in the British Isles. This was all so sudden, and slightly mysterious. Was I walking into some James Bond plot? Two weeks later, Susan and Allan joined Lorna and me for lunch. Lorna would manage the restaurant if we moved forward. The lunch was more a mutual sizing up than a business meeting. Susan and Allan rolled in with a Porsche SUV—a promising sign for a Porsche fan like me. Allan climbed out in corduroys, a plaid shirt, and loafers—casual attire for a British billionaire my age.

He wasn't there just to make small talk. He took in the restaurant's design, commenting on details like the silverware and table arrangement. He complimented the atmosphere and asked how I "put things together." I shrugged and admitted, "I shamelessly borrow ideas from places I've visited." He chuckled, and I knew we'd get along.

When we finally arrived at the River Islands site, I was floored. This was the largest development I'd ever seen. River Islands is an eight-square-mile community along the San Joaquin Delta, about sixty miles east of both San Francisco and Silicon Valley. River Islands Development, part of the Cambay Group, started it in the early 2000s. By late 2024, partners like Kiper Homes, Lennar, TRI Pointe Homes, and Del Webb had built nearly five thousand houses. By 2045, the community would boast fifteen thousand homes, schools, shops, parks, and sports facilities, with forty thousand people calling it home—a mix of families, empty nesters, and active retirees. River Islands didn't build houses directly; it developed roads, approved house plans, and managed its own lots. River Islands handled the infrastructure and amenities to satisfy builders and future residents alike.

Over the following weeks, Susan became my collaborator on what was shaping up to be my biggest project since selling the construction company. Even as our lawyers hashed out a contract, she looped me into meetings with people who'd work on the proposed Redwood Café at River Islands. Her team suggested a prime lakeside lot in a commercial area that would serve as the heart of the community. Her engineers proposed cutting the Modesto restaurant into thirds and trucking it over in the dead of night. She introduced me to Doug Dahlin, founder of the Dahlin Group, the renowned architecture firm behind River Islands's master plan. Doug was still involved, weighing in on every new detail.

Doug impressed me. He'd come out of semi-retirement for this project, energized by the chance to collaborate. He explained that River Islands wanted a vibrant village center. Since COVID-19, drawing people into these spaces had become a global challenge. But Doug had a theory: Restaurants could still pull people in. Once they were there, they'd explore the rest. Doug wanted to create a restaurant experience beyond the usual chains. He noted how Restoration Hardware had started adding restaurants to their showrooms, using dining to anchor a space. Any national chain could've moved in here, but River Islands needed something to appeal to the well-traveled, upscale residents they wanted to attract—even those from the Bay Area. Allan, a wine aficionado with a high-end vineyard in Napa, wasn't about to settle for an Olive Garden. Dahlin could handle the structure, Doug said, "but we need you to give it the feel." Flattery's a powerful motivator, and I couldn't believe someone of his caliber wanted my input on a project this big. "I'm ready to get started," I told him.

In meetings over the next weeks, I understood why they needed me. They had highly trained professionals at their beck and call, but American housing had become homogenized; developments all looked the same. The complexity of building codes meant that once developers found an approved plan, they stuck with it to avoid bureaucratic hassle. This trend stripped away all uniqueness. European towns brimmed with eclectic, historic buildings, but California's new developments were interchangeable, whether in Los Angeles, Fresno, or Modesto. Slap a grocery store in the middle, add a mall, and you never knew one from the next.

Susan and Allan wanted to break the mold, and they were willing to put real money behind the effort. They believed I could provide the touch they desired. Susan's visit to my restaurant in Patterson confirmed that I wasn't a one-hit wonder. The Patterson location looked nothing like the Modesto one, yet each had a unique, high-quality feel. Susan and Allan were interested in more than just a restaurant—they wanted my ideas and sensibility. I would oversee the interior design, decor, exterior landscaping, lighting, and more. It wouldn't stop with the restaurant. When Susan returned from Cambay's annual board meeting in Abu Dhabi in September, she immediately called and said she wanted to discuss their Napa winery plans. She said, "We need to get you over there."

There's a lesson here: Over the years, we build up a pile of skills, often so gradually that we forget how valuable they are. These skills don't just improve what we do for current clients—they open doors we might not have thought to knock on. I'd built up my design instincts the old-fashioned way, by paying attention. I'd met people from all walks of life—forklift drivers, heart surgeons, nuclear scientists, winemakers. Their homes and gardens gave me endless ideas. Many had hired top-tier designers, so I saw world-class work up close. Over years of conversations, projects, and travels worldwide, I had built a mental catalog of what worked and what didn't. Eventually, when the time was right, I put those lessons to work.

At our first meeting in Patterson, Susan had said, "Allan and I make all the decisions, and we make them fast." I thought, *Yeah, I've heard that before.* But she delivered. Boom—offer on the table. Boom—lawyers deployed. Boom—the billionaire shows up. Boom—the project gets an upgrade. Boom—world-class architects join the team. It was boom, boom, boom, all within sixty to ninety days. What would've taken most people a year, Susan handled in months. Most people stall, analyze, and agonize over every decision. Her decisiveness set the tone, pushing everyone to keep up. It motivated me to make things happen too.

The first week in October, I signed a contract to move the Redwood Café to River Islands by early 2025, with me overseeing operations for five years. Lorna would manage it, as well as the Old Water House. We held a signing ceremony in Susan's office. She filmed it on her phone, officially marking the start of our partnership. I half joked about my "indentured servitude." I promised to document the relocation process on video—bulldozers clearing the new Redwood site, the Modesto building being disassembled and rebuilt at its new home. I'd post the videos on my YouTube channel, so the River Islands community could follow along. Six months ago, I was riding off into the sunset, and now? I was back at it, full speed ahead.

In mid-October, I walked my youngest daughter, Caroline, down the aisle at a wedding at our home. Three days later, Lynna and I traveled to Sicily with a small group of friends, led by our trusty guide, Davide. Then we headed to Istanbul, stopping at Dracul's castle in Slovakia. It was a sort of working second honeymoon; we scouted future tour locations. After that, I rolled up my sleeves and dove into River Islands.

Over time, I'd assembled a network of trusted vendors and craftsmen, each contributing to various projects. They handled various projects around my house and yard, and I deployed them for outside jobs, like the Patterson restaurant.

While I was knee-deep in River Islands, they were busily building a helicopter hangar for an Enstrom Shark I'd picked up at the beginning of the year. Despite loudly declaring I was "done with flying forever," apparently "forever" meant about five years. Like quitting smoking, swearing off flying was noble in theory but trickier in practice. I thought about the grueling hours, the piles of cash, and the bruised ego it took to get that hard-won license. I still had my health—and enough marbles—so I figured I was no danger to myself or anyone else.

The Shark sat on a farm in Pennsylvania; it took two and a half months to find someone willing to dismantle the blades, load it on a trailer, and haul it across the country. Once it arrived, I reattached the blades and got back in the air.

But a single taste of flying didn't cut it. When I heard another Beechcraft Bonanza was for sale, I didn't think twice before writing a check. I imagined myself on cross-country flights, inspired by my friend Donnie Monaco, who'd flown his V35 Bonanza from Florida at my age. I had friends all over the country, and dropping in on them sounded like the perfect adventure.

As I took to the skies, the familiar hum of the engine felt like reuniting with an old friend. The world shrank into a neat checkerboard of greens and browns, and it struck me that this was an apt metaphor for my life. It was never just about getting somewhere—it was also about the journey.

In the spring of 2024, I was gassing up the Enstrom at the Oakdale airport when a tall, dark-haired guy in his fifties climbed out of a huge helicopter parked by a hangar. The building had *Helius* plastered on it, and through the open door, I could see a fleet of gorgeous helicopters lined up. These weren't your average birds; they were sleek, top-notch machines used for high-stakes missions, the kind of choppers that make you stand a little straighter just looking at them. Way out of my league.

The guy waved me over. "Hey, I'm Rooster," he said in a thick Cajun drawl, eyeing my Enstrom. "Cute little machine." We chatted about the weather, and before I knew it, he was inviting me inside.

We ended up standing next to a gleaming MD 600—an unmistakable model thanks to the no-tail-rotor design that uses rotor wash to keep it steady. He tapped its side. "This is what you need," he said. "You can make money with it." I laughed it off. Then he said, "You need to meet my boss." I shrugged, thinking he was kidding. "Sure, anytime."

Two days later, I got a call from John Stonecipher, Helius's owner. He and his wife were in town from Arizona and wanted to meet. Over lunch at the Redwood Café, John got right to it. Helius had a contract with PG&E for remote line maintenance and needed a Bell 407 to do the job. A used one was coming out of rehab in Canada—price tag: a couple million bucks. "We're hoping you'll buy the helicopter and lease it to us."

Now, I may not be the sharpest knife in the drawer, but I'm no fool, either. I dug into their spreadsheets and proposals and had my eagle-eyed lawyer and accountant give them the once-over, and they liked what they saw. This type of private sale-leaseback arrangement was common enough and packed plenty of perks—steady cash flow, profits, tax breaks. PG&E would lease the chopper from Helius and maintain it to their own strict standards, with only top-rated pilots flying it. In short, PG&E was the safety net.

One thing about an entrepreneurial mindset: The wheels never stop turning. I was constantly looking at things from different angles, hunting for new opportunities. How could I use my Helius connection to add value at River Islands? I was like an unfiltered idea machine, bringing up suggestions no one else in the River Islands organization would've dared mention. It wasn't every day someone said, "Hey, let's buy a $2.5 million helicopter" in a boardroom meeting. That's risky territory. Bosses tended to be shielded from unconventional ideas, only seeing the ones that had been triple-checked and deemed "safe" by their teams.

I had no such filter. I told Susan, "Imagine this: When Allan lands in his private jet, a helicopter could pick him up right from the tarmac and take him directly to where he needs to be. Total luxury. Why not offer chopper trips from River Islands to his Napa vineyard?" I'd asked John and Kathy from Helius if this kind of service was in their wheelhouse. They normally raked in $5,000 an hour on high-risk utility jobs, but as a valued partner, John said they'd be game to support River Islands. "If they buy a helicopter, we'll maintain it, fly it, handle whatever they need," he said.

Unlike my new helicopter—which was locked in an exclusive-use contract with PG&E for their operations—a River Islands helicopter would be available for other work. This meant Helius could use it when River Islands didn't need it. Say a fire broke out in Fresno, and Cal Fire needed emergency transport; Helius could deploy the River Islands helicopter, charging Cal Fire a solid $14,000 for the job. If they logged sixty hours a year with that chopper, it would more than pay for itself.

Flying to Napa would require some finesse, though. Napa had strict restrictions, so we'd need a variance to get landing permissions, navigating local politics along the way. John thought he could make a strong case by emphasizing the community benefits, like firefighting support. Once we had clearance, the possibilities were endless. Imagine a direct flight from River Islands to a Napa winery in under an hour—wine dinners with helicopter transport back to River Islands, creating a luxury experience few others could offer.

Susan liked the idea. She mentioned Del Webb was building nine hundred homes aimed at affluent, active, fifty-five-plus buyers—people who were financially secure and looking for more than just a place to live. "They want to know what they'll be able to do: hiking trails, wine tastings, travel clubs, you name it," she said. "I told Del Webb about your travel company, and they suggested we set up a Del Webb River Islands travel club." My entrepreneurial gears started spinning. Del Webb could hand deliver a pool of ready-made customers to Redwood Tours. Every buyer would get a membership card, opening up travel options curated just for them.

I imagined trips from River Islands to Napa for wine tastings, with a helicopter departure at 5:30 p.m., a chef's dinner at the winery, and a return flight by 9 p.m., landing within walking distance of home. It would be a one thousand-dollar experience—helicopter ride, sunset over the Delta, coastal range views. One catch, though: Would Somerston Vineyard be able to install a helipad? Napa was a mixed bag on helicopters. Some vineyards used them for frost protection or quick transport during harvest, but plenty of locals wanted them grounded. John said we could play up the law enforce-ment angle, which might help sway things. At the end of 2024, the River Islands helicopter idea was still on the table, but I was optimistic that I could make it a reality.

Meanwhile, Susan mentioned River Islands didn't have a YouTube channel and asked if I'd produce one. As soon as we signed the con-tract, her marketing team handed me a list of forty-two videos they wanted for the restaurant campaign and offered to pay the going rate. Knowing agency prices, I saw the potential for a nice profit. Plus, River Islands planned to share the videos with thousands of homeowners and prospective buyers. Some of them might check out my *GetBack2Work!* channel, boosting traffic across my own brand. The YouTube investment was shaping up to pay off.

None of this would've been possible without an arsenal of connections.

River Islands offered me something rare: a chance to create something that would outlast me. Designing a restaurant, maybe a Napa winery, even adding public art to the landscape—this let me contribute to a legacy. Years from now, when I'm long gone, people might encounter my work, may even be influenced by it. That idea stirred something deep. It was a curious satisfaction, knowing that part of me might live on in these projects. Not everyone gets to shape a place, to leave a legacy in stone and steel. But there, in that work, I'd found a way to do just that.

Looking back on when I started working on this book, I asked myself: *What lessons have I really learned? What advice could I offer to both budding and seasoned entrepreneurs navigating their own chaotic paths?* After all, every business is unique, every industry its own beast.

Times change; technology reshapes the playing field; the economy rises, falls, and does a few pirouettes along the way. But as I began exploring my past, my family, and the businesses I had built, I realized I did have plenty of hard-won lessons to impart through my story, which I hope has resonated with you. Ultimately, there's no formula, no foolproof recipe you can rely on to become a successful entrepreneur. But I have found the following bits of wisdom hold true above all others:

**Curiosity is everything.** Stay curious—about people, industries, problems, and, yes, even about your mistakes. It's your compass through uncharted territory. I learned more from asking questions (and making mistakes) than from any business manual.

**Adaptability is survival.** The ability to pivot is a survival skill in business, like water to a sailor. If your first restaurant concept flops, get back in the kitchen, reimagine the menu, or rethink the atmosphere. Your success often depends on how quickly you can change course without losing your sense of direction.

**Persistence beats talent.** You don't need to be a born genius to succeed. You do, however, need to outlast most other people. I wasn't the most gifted salesperson, but I kept showing up, learning, and refining my approach.

**Seek wisdom, not just knowledge.** Books, mentors, and even tough competitors can teach you more than any conference ever could. You'll find some of the best lessons in unexpected places—like the pilot who taught me the discipline of helicopter flight, which turned out to apply to business more than I'd ever imagined.

**Embrace the mess.** Business isn't a neat and tidy series of chapters. It's a stew, a bouillabaisse, with ingredients mixing in unpredictable ways. Each endeavor you take on, each failure and success, will inevitably shape the next. Embrace it, or at least don't try too hard to sort it all out. Life's too interesting to live in straight lines.

# About the Authors

**Robert "Bob" Campana** is a California builder, landscape designer, real estate developer, restaurateur, and all-round serial entrepreneur. Born in San Francisco, he grew up in the Sierra Nevada foothills. At age twenty, he quit his job on a backwoods survey crew to travel the world, a journey that changed his life. Returning to California, he started a small business manufacturing and installing redwood hot tubs and eventually grew the company into one of the state's premier swimming pool builders. He later launched and acquired several other successful ventures, including Modesto's popular Redwood Café, which Yelp calls "one of America's most romantic restaurants." In 2022, he created Redwood Café Tours to develop luxury small-group adventures in Europe, Asia, and Oceania. An experienced helicopter and airplane pilot, he travels the world and celebrates life with his wife, Lynna.

**Niles Howard** is a business journalist, editor, and author. A Northwestern University graduate, he has held senior positions at *Inc.* and *Money* magazines and with other major media companies. He advises investment, law, and consulting firms on communications and marketing.